MW01171850

# Relationship Real Estate

# Relationship Real Estate

## 16 Steps to Real Estate Success

Tina Valiant

Relationship Real Estate: 16 Steps to Real Estate Success


Disclaimer:

The author strives to be as accurate and complete as possible in the creation of this book, notwithstanding the fact that the author does not warrant or represent at any time that the contents within are accurate due to the rapidly changing nature of the Internet.

While all attempts have been made to verify information provided in this publication, the Author and the Publisher assume no responsibility and are not liable for errors, omissions, or contrary interpretation of the subject matter herein. The Author and Publisher hereby disclaim any liability, loss or damage incurred as a result of the application and utilization, whether directly or indirectly, of any information, suggestion, advice, or procedure in this book. Any perceived slights of specific persons, peoples, or organizations are unintentional.

In practical advice books, like anything else in life, there are no guarantees of income made. Readers are cautioned to rely on their own judgment about their individual circumstances to act accordingly. Readers are responsible for their own actions, choices, and results. This book is not intended for use as a source of legal, business, accounting or financial advice. All readers are advised to seek the services of competent professionals in legal, business, accounting, and finance field.

Printed in the United States of America

ISBN: 978-1-948382-31-1 paperback
JMP2022.2

# Contents

# 1

# How I Ended Up Here

I have been in real estate almost twenty plus years in different capacities. In 2001, I accepted a position with Starwood Vacation Ownership, yes Timeshare sales, not knowing anything about sales or what a timeshare was. Through the course of my two-week training class, I learned scripts, the process of the sale, and personality profiling. Product knowledge was secondary as my eyes were opened to a whole new world of sales and drawing emotion out of our "guests".

Those that know me now find it hard to believe I was voted least likely to succeed in my training class of eleven. I didn't look the part because I had a "stay-at-home mom" wardrobe and hair. I had to borrow clothes from a friend to go to work every day for the first month of my employment. I didn't know the first thing about sales or the product. I certainly did not act like the other sales people, nor did I party like them. What I did have that nobody anticipated was determination. I was in a situation at home that I could not leave because I would not be able to take care of myself and my two young daughters financially. The only way I was going to succeed in finding my freedom was to learn this business and excel at it!

As the other sales associates sat in the back room, mingling and playing cards waiting for their turn on the floor, I was finding anything and everything I could to learn and master my craft. First, I recorded myself saying the scripts and would listen to them over and over again. They became such a second nature to me that I can still verbally deliver them to this day, almost 20 years later. As I finally began receiving tours with guests, the language Starwood wanted me to use was natural and free flowing. The steps of the sale were built into the script so that I didn't have to think about it. Secondly, I constantly read sales books that were recommended to me by my management team. I couldn't figure out why I was still not selling?

As I looked around the back room at the ones that were selling, I kept thinking "if they can do this then so can I!" I began going to my closing managers after every tour and asking them what I could have done differently. They seemed to enjoy my desire to learn, and it seemed to feed their ego to teach me. They all had different styles, but the same recommendation kept surfacing; Sales are always created by emotion and backed by logic. It became clear that I was not evoking emotion. In order to be successful at this new career, I had to figure out how to evoke the emotion needed to close a sale. As I went through my discovery questions with one of the closing managers, he looked at me and made a profound statement; "Tina, you are an emotional person. Tap into the "why" behind the answers your guests give you and pull from your emotion to help them understand that they are left with a loss if they do not buy this product to fulfill their why." Before that exact moment, I realized I had been pitching product and not tapping into the people and why they were on vacation while I was meeting with them. Somewhere in them, it must be important, or they wouldn't be on vacation to begin with!

One of the things they taught us in training was that 1 in 10 people buy from you regardless of how well you did on your presentation. If you could sell 2 in 10, you were a Rockstar. If you could sell 3 in 10, you reached the level of superstar status! I aimed to be a superstar and yet here I was going out on my seventh tour with no sale yet. It was time for me to shine and evoke emotion because that was what I was missing. I had to make them feel a loss if they said no. Not because of pressure or words I was saying, but because of their words and what they were saying.

I greeted my guests, went through the script, began discovery, and focused on everything they said while writing down their answers. When I got to questions where I could ask why they felt that way, I didn't hesitate. My discovery lasted longer than usual, but what I understood made it worth it. As I was showing them the product and how it fit into their why, they seemed to get excited. By the end, they were asking me how much this was going to cost them. They were not able to purchase that day because they could not work it into their budget, but they felt a loss and were sad about it.

After that presentation, I understood what I had been missing in my presentations and continued evoking emotion. My eighth tour purchased a package and so did my ninth. After that, I became a 3 in 10 closer and continued learning more about my craft of sales. By the second month, I was the only one left from my training class and was in the top 10% of the resort, employing 268 sales associates. I eventually became a sales trainer in Vacation Ownership as I began understanding the psychology behind all of the sales steps.

Later, I left Vacation Ownership sales to build law office Foreclosure Defense departments in the crash of the market. My responsibilities included designing defenses, building and implementing systems for short sale and loan modification negotiations, hiring and training the negotiation teams, and bringing in all of the clients through relationships with realtors. I chose this profession because I wanted to be a voice for those that didn't have one and wanted to make a difference. I had no idea that my sales background and understanding the psychology behind sales techniques would come in so handy. In the Foreclosure world, I had a 90% closing ratio with the clients and a 100% track record in negotiating loans through short sales and loan modifications. I maintained my closing ratios for ten years in the Foreclosure world. I don't believe there are many situations in life more emotional than losing one's home. I was able to utilize my understanding of the emotions behind my client's "why" and successfully open the lender's eyes to their stories. My clients became people to the lenders instead of numbers. It was not uncommon for the negotiators with the lenders to jump through hoops in order to help my clients and me.

During my time with the law offices, I maintained my real estate license and dabbled here and there as a referral agent. While with my last attorney employer, he had me utilize my license for different things. On top of managing the foreclosure department, I also was mentored by him on bringing residential and commercial properties to highest and best use. I managed his residential and commercial portfolio, found great deals for him in both arenas of real estate, and managed his contractors for renovations on the properties he purchased. He allowed me to explore other avenues of income, including off market commercial and the EB-5 Immigration program.

Another responsibility I was given was building business plans for various types of companies he was interested in opening. I built five business models for various real estate related companies. His passion was all things real estate. He had a desire to eventually quit practicing law, and just focus on his real estate dreams. I designed a real estate brokerage business model, title, concierge property management, note purchasing, and an office suites management company. Every time he asked me to put a business plan together, I was ecstatic! I was always hopeful he would implement at least one of them. To my frustration, he never did.

Meanwhile, my real estate referral business was really taking off. I was getting to the point of having two to four transactions close a month. I always had thoughts of being a realtor but my "friends" that I was giving my referrals to told me that I would never make it as a real estate agent. They said I didn't have the patience or the knowhow. They said it would take me too long to learn. I don't know why I believed them, but I did. For a long time, I just kept giving them to my clients and collecting my referral fees.

The day my previous attorney employer and I parted ways was the day my life would change in business. I don't think I would have left him on my own. I felt such loyalty towards him for all that I had learned in my almost four years with him. Just recently, he explained that he knew I would never leave so he pushed me out of the nest. It was time for me to fly! As I look back on my time with him, I remember being so frustrated that he never implemented anything that he had me build.

Later I realized he had me build the variety of company business plans for me. Inadvertently, he gave me the tools to build my own empire because he recognized how my mind worked and wanted me to be able to soar. He laid the foundations of building business models and as I built them, he knew I would narrow down what I enjoyed and didn't enjoy about each model.

After parting ways, I floundered for a bit, not knowing which direction to go. I began working with foreclosure properties, wholesalers, and flippers. Because of the knowledge I had built, I understood wholesaling and flipping quite well. Florida is a pretty wholesale friendly state, but not all states are created equal in that world. I was still kind of holding myself back from residential real estate because of the negative voices still being around me.

One day, I had a very clear vision that hit me like a two-by-four! All of a sudden, I saw the empire that I was to build. I remember having a conversation with my boyfriend at the time. I told him that we were going to build a real estate empire together and that he needed to get his life in order because he was not ready. What I didn't tell him was that the empire was not in Florida in my vision. I accepted the vision, but I fought it. I was surrounded by "takers' in my life that wanted to extract all that was in my head.

My boyfriend, who later became my husband for a short period of time, made a deal for partnership in finding properties to wholesale and flip. In the negotiation, I was the commodity. My role would be to build and implement all of the knowledge I had into a business model that could become national. I felt like I was sold to be placed in an office while others extracted everything out of me. After about six weeks and a crazy series of events, I pulled myself out of the deal. The series of events and betrayals that followed from many I knew for a long period of time paralyzed me for a couple of months. My desire and passion for real estate was stolen from me and I was lost.

I remember it like it was yesterday, the day I decided to take back my life. June 11, 2016, I looked at my boyfriend and explained I was moving to Arizona the following Sunday. He could go or he could stay, but I was leaving. I sold everything in my apartment in four days, shipped my clothes to my parents, and left the following weekend. My boyfriend decided to move as well, but I was hesitant. Through our ten-day journey across the country, I felt my dark cloud lift. I still had not decided if real estate would be my profession, and that was okay. All I knew was the possibilities were endless.

Once in Arizona, I went through my real estate broker's class and passed my tests. I left my license inactive and tried a couple of professions. After six months, and pressure from my boyfriend, I leaped into real estate in January of 2017. I didn't know anybody except my family and had no savings. My boyfriend quit his job with a steady income, and I literally had six weeks to make a paycheck or we would be homeless. Again, I had something that cannot be taught in a classroom, determination!

We door knocked, found other agents to allow me to do open houses for them, started a networking group in Scottsdale, and began introducing myself to vendors. While holding my second open house, I sold the home to one of the visitors. The closing happened literally two days prior to my bills being due. I kept going, kept pushing, working 6 to 7 days a week. I made every mistake in the book at first, but that didn't matter. I pushed the negative voices out of my head and kept focused on getting more clients and meeting more people.

By April, I was at eight properties either closed or in escrow. Things were moving and I felt like I was finally getting to know the valley. I hired my first team member and thus began the beginning of The Valiant Team. My boyfriend, not husband yet, was doing well and was very helpful with the marketing and helping my stepson put out open house signs. We were on our way to my vision, but not without some stumbling blocks along the way.

My foot had been broken in January, literally two weeks after I activated my license. The fall caused my L5/S1 disc in my lower back to completely herniate, pinching off my left sciatic nerve. I had lower back surgery in April of 2017, the same day my eighth property was closing. Because of the medications prior to the back surgery, I ended up in the ER in May with severe diverticulitis.

Through it all, I kept pushing and by July had seven team members. In October, my husband of eight months started drinking again and began pulling back from being helpful. I kept pushing through, even though my heart was broken, and I knew what was coming on a personal level. I hired my full-time assistant to help pick up the slack where my husband was not helping anymore, and by the end of the year closed 42 properties and was nominated Rookie of the Year valley wide by the Arizona Business Journal.

In 2018, we changed brokerages to a better fee structure for my team, which of course meant rebranding signs and everything else. I lost three team members in the transition and was left with four and my assistant. Our goal was 100 transactions and a volume of $25,000,000. The obstacles continued as I had to have knee surgery from the fall the previous year and a full bowel resection in December of 2018. I began divorce proceedings and rebranded my team to the Tkay Group in September of 2018. My team never skipped a beat as we pushed towards our goal. By January of 2019, our numbers were finalized at 100 closed transactions and a volume of $26,400,000! Myself and my team won several awards for 2018, proving that my systems and training worked!

My purpose for explaining all of this to you is so that you can first understand my background but also so that you can see that success in Real Estate can be accomplished through hard work and dedication, no matter what your obstacles. We are in a new age of Real Estate where paying for lead generation is not the answer to your success. Real Estate has become more about relationships than ever before. With flat fee brokerages, large companies offering cash with quick closes, and the internet trying to push realtors out, you must be smarter about the industry. You must be willing to work face to face with people and excel at the customer service you offer. You must be able to show value to your potential clients for your services! The days of just sticking a sign in the yard for your listings are long gone!

When interviewing potential team members, they must show me that they are not just in it for the money, rather they have a desire to be a contribution and help people. My motto is “if you do right by people, the money will come on its own.” This book will explain the psychology behind why my team does and says the things they do. I will walk you through how to be an asset to your clients and how to build lasting relationships. I will teach you how to be different from other real estate agents and give a higher level of service to your clients. You will have a road map for your success.

Those that believe they are getting into real estate because they want to set their own hours and have a flexible schedule will more than likely stay at the average realtor's income of $25,000 and maybe three or four closings their first, second and third year. If you want to make six figures and have a desire to make real estate a long-term career, I will help you get there. There will be times that you are uncomfortable and may even doubt your ability to do this! In order to be successful, you must first become uncomfortable! If you persevere, you will get there!

This book is being written by request from several in the industry. I have been warned by naysayers not to share my "secrets". I laugh when this is said to me because there are no tricks up my sleeve that I am unveiling! In my opinion, this is knowledge that should be shared with all who want to learn. Yes, I have combined my vacation ownership sales experience, legal/negotiation experience, and real estate into one program that has clearly led to success. It is my pleasure to share it with you!

# 2

# Mindset

Mindset and how we perceive everything in life means the difference between those that are successful and those that are not. Throughout this chapter we will be looking at why you chose real estate. What are you hoping to gain? Most importantly, and I cannot stress this enough, we are going to look at how you need to keep your attitude and your surrounding strong. At the end of the day, it all comes down to your belief system and removing your limiting beliefs from your mind and spirit.

So, why did you choose real estate as your profession? Was it an idea that popped into your head on a whim, life circumstance, or did it just look like fun to you? Whatever the case may be, real estate can be a fun and rewarding profession. There will be challenges and frustrations along the way that you must learn to overcome. There will be moments when you realize real estate is not what you expected at all! There will also be days that you feel exhilarated and full of excitement because of the difference you are making in people's lives.

Let's first look at the myths of a real estate career. If you have gotten into real estate because you thought it would be easy with big money potential, you are in for a shock! The word "easy" does not exist in real estate. If you thought you would be able to set your own schedule and maybe work less but make more money, you chose the wrong profession! Sometimes, you will be pushed beyond your limits in exhaustion. There may have been thoughts that you have a ton of friends and family that will refer you. Sadly, they may not refer to you because you are a friend or family member. Do you fit into the categories above? Don't worry, everybody does at first!

What does a real estate career really look like? Especially in the beginning, you will work long hours. You will be at the beck and call of your clients and their schedules. Every transaction is different as well as every client. No two transactions are the same. There will be obstacles to overcome. You will have to become a problem solver, counselor, the voice for those that don't have one, and the master of your product and area. In some cases, you will have to think like an attorney, become an expert negotiator, and be a bulldog on behalf of your clients when needed. These are the things that nobody tells you when seeking a real estate career.

Now, take a deep breath and exhale. Let me open your eyes to one of the most rewarding careers out there. There is no better feeling than when you find your clients the perfect home and they walk in and squeal "this is it!" You will be helping clients that are going through transitions of their life. Maybe a spouse or loved one passed away. Maybe the kids have all gone to college or gotten married and your client needs to downsize while going through the "empty nest" feelings of sadness. Occasionally, your clients will be divorcing and needing to liquidate their assets. Whatever the transitions in their lives may be, you are their angel, guiding them through, holding their hands, and personally walking them through to the next chapter of their lives. Real estate is about relationships.

Whether you have been in sales before or not, being successful in real estate is and has to be about the people you will touch every day. You have the opportunity to make a difference in their lives. What can be more rewarding than that? Along with taking care of others, their hopes and dreams, you must also realize and remember your hopes and dreams. What will real estate do for you? It all has to do with your mindset and your purpose.

As I mentioned in the previous chapter, back in my Vacation Ownership days, remember all of the salespeople sitting in the back room? What do you think most of them were doing? They were sitting in the back room, gossiping, playing cards, filling themselves with self-doubt, and not growing their mind. Vacation Ownership is a cut throat industry and every month the companies let go of several people that did not make their goals. The saying was "you are only as good as the month you are in". I will never forget the day the company fired a gentleman that had been number two in sales three months in a row and then had a bad month. He was gone just like that!

I realized very quickly I could not and would not be like the other sales people sitting there doing absolutely nothing. They automatically started speaking negatively about me saying I was stuck up and unfriendly. They could tell I was different, and they didn't like it. I was listening to books on audio regarding sales. I was spending time with my closing managers, picking their brain on how I could improve. My mind was set that I was going to be a superstar and I was protective of who I would let near me. I wasn't there to make friends with the sales people. I was there to own my world and thrive in it! I was there to gain my freedom!

Your mindset is what you should be most protective of because it will dictate everything moving forward. You must be careful who you allow into your inner circle because they are the ones that influence your thoughts. If you are surrounded by negative or complacent people, you will inevitably become negative and complacent. If you surround yourself with successful and positive people, you will inevitably become successful and positive. It is the law of attraction, scientifically proven to exist. What you put out into the world, you will receive.

I was recently having a life coaching session with a friend of mine in another state. After speaking to him for some time, it became clear I was going to need some reinforcement. I called another friend of mine to come over and hop on a call with me. My friend in another state was battling his mindset. He knew he needed to change his surroundings, but also the negative influences in his life. He felt it made him look arrogant or better than those around him to begin distancing himself. My reinforcement friend came up with an analogy I see as priceless!

## The Bed Bug Theory

If you don't know about bed bugs, let me first explain them. Bed bugs infest a home and are impossible to get rid of. It only takes one bed bug to infest your home. If you had a family member or friend and you knew they had bed bugs, knowing it only takes one being on their body or clothes, to infest your home, would you let them through the door? No! Absolutely not! You would be kind and loving, but explain to them that you have to love them from a distance until their situation is clear and the bed bugs are gone.

Now, look at the people in your life that are negative and/or complacent. Negative thoughts and complacency should be looked at like bed bugs. You must protect your mindset at all cost! It only takes one person in your life to be negative or complacent and infest your mind, goals, and dreams. You must kindly love these people from a distance and not allow them to infest your mindset. If there are those types of people in your life currently, it is time to exterminate. This does not mean you cannot be friends with them, but you must choose to love them from a distance in order to reach your full potential.

One of the most important rules in successful sales is surrounding yourself with like-minded individuals who have the same belief systems and aspirations as you.

Another mindset we need to squash is from our own industry. There is somewhat of a mass panic going on in our industry right now. We have large conglomerates coming in to our markets making cash offers on homes as well as flat fee listing companies. The world of technology has opened the door wide for these types of companies to exist. Companies like Open Door and Purple Brick have come into the industry offering a quick sale of consumers homes. Realtors who have the gloom and doom mindset fear these companies will make real estate agents obsolete. They love talking about it and using these companies as an excuse for their lack of success. Zillow and Redfin are opening their own brokerages country wide and charging real estate agents not only thousands of dollars for lead generation, but also referral fees for clients given.

I am explaining all of this to you so that you can battle the negative mindset on these topics. The reason that my team has been successful through the shift happening in our industry is because we are relationship based. No matter what technology has to offer in real estate, there will always be clients who desire a live person to take care of them and have their best interest at heart. The biggest problem with the large technology conglomerates is they charge hefty fees to the clients, give them offers for their properties that are much less than what the properties should retail for, and have very little customer service.

There will be times that you lose a potential client to one of these companies, however more times than not your potential clients will find value in utilizing your services because of the relationship you have built with them. There are valuable lessons you will learn throughout this book building rapport and showing quality service that will enable you to win over technology-based companies the majority of the time. My team has only lost two potential clients over the past four years to these entities. They do not scare us because we are different!

Lastly, you should be feeding your mind on a regular basis. Whether you are an audio or paper person, books are waiting for you. We are not reinventing the wheel of real estate or sales. Why not begin studying your craft so that you can master it? I have my own library of books that I check out to my team. "The Psychology of Selling" by Brian Tracey is one of my favorites to recommend. The book changed my thought process in sales twenty-plus years ago. I will continue carrying a copy of it today. "The Traveler's Gift" by Andy Andrews is another favorite. I live by the "Seven Decisions" from Andrews' book on a daily basis. I read them regularly and my team all have a copy of them.

Whether it be sharpening your tools to master your craft or retraining your brain to focus on the positives of life, we have so many resources to learn from those that have walked before us. There are also motivational videos, podcasts, blogs and anything else you can think of to increase your brain power and thoughts. In real estate, lazy is not an option, at least not if you want to excel at it!

Understanding how important your mindset is and being protective of your environment and surroundings is the absolute first level in creating your foundation for a rewarding career in real estate. Understanding what a real estate career really looks like instead of the myths you have believed is just the beginning. Ignoring the naysayer press, friends and family that want to unintentionally steal your fire is essential for your long-term success. And lastly, surrounding yourself with like-minded people who share your passion and drive, while feeding your minds with more knowledge and positivity is an equation equaling success. You are on your way to a rewarding and beneficial career in real estate!

# 3

# Setting Goals

Twenty years ago, I learned the value of setting my goals and writing them down. I can't remember who said it that far back, but the statement was "when you write down your goals, the likelihood of you hitting them is much higher." When you read books from sales gurus like Brian Tracy and many others, they always emphasize setting your goals and writing them down. I have spent many years utilizing this concept and teaching it to others. I can say with absolute certainty that it works; however, we must dive into why it works!

Goals are the constant reminder of our vision for our life. When I write out my goals every December and January, I not only focus on where I want to be, but I also evaluate if I hit my target the previous year. Writing our goals gives us a roadmap for the coming year and keeps us on track throughout the year. Our goals should be in front of us regularly to ensure we are focused and following the path we set for ourselves.

Although many people write out their professional goals, you should also be writing out your personal and spiritual goals. I also recommend having not only a yearly goal, but also a two-year plan and a five-year plan. Clearly, your long-term goals can change depending on the path your life takes, but having a roadmap of hopes and dreams is an essential part of continued success. It can sometimes become your driving force to keep moving forward in the midst of setbacks and obstacles.

## Career Goals:

In real estate, you must first decide what you want to make as far as income. Most people I have spoken to, as well as myself, start with a goal of wanting to make six figures. In real estate, six figures are definitely obtainable. What most people do not account for is the expense of conducting business. In real estate, there are many expenses associated with conducting business. An expense budget must be established before you can determine how much you need to Gross in order to hit your Net income goal. Below are expenses that must be considered:

1. Brokerage Fees
2. Licensing Fees
3. Board Fees
4. Listing Signs
5. Open House Signs
6. Lock Boxes
7. Listing Fees such as photos and sign placement
8. Customer Relations Management System (CRM)
9. Website
10. Closing Gifts
11. Additional Marketing

12. Printing
13. Transaction Coordination

The goal is to keep your costs of doing business to about 30% of your Gross Income. Let's say your goal is to Net $100,000. If you factor your expenses to 30%, your Gross Commission Income (GCI) goal needs to be roughly $145,000. This number is taking into consideration if you are at a 100% brokerage where you pay a transaction fee. If you are at a brokerage that takes a percentage of your commission, Your GCI needs to be higher to account for the brokerage fees.

The next step is determining how many transactions you need to close in order to hit your targeted GCI. Let's say you are at a 100% brokerage and your transaction fee is $299.00. The average transaction in your area is $300,000 and your market average commission rate is 3%.

$300,000 x 3% = $9,000 GCI

$9,000 - $299 Brokerage Fee = $8,701 Net Commission

$145,000 / $8,701 = 16.7 Transactions

In this scenario, $145,000 would be the commission you bring home. Our allowance for marketing would be about $45,000 and your net would be just over $100,000. The $100,000 is what you would be paying taxes on, so it is important to have your tax plan arranged as well.

Another scenario is working for a brokerage that takes a percentage of your commission, hopefully because of the training and services they provide. Many brokerages take 30% of your commission. Let's look at how this affects your transaction goals:

$300,000 x 3% = $9,000 GCI

$9,000 x 30% = $2,700 Brokerage Fee

$9,000 - $2,700 = $6,300 Net Commission

$145,000 / $6,300 = 23 Transactions

In this scenario, 23 transactions are what you need to bring home, $145,000 per year. Your marketing expenses of 30%, equaling $45,000, is used for marketing your business and your $100,000 is your net income you will report to the IRS.

There is no right or wrong answer as to what type of brokerage is best for you. Brokerages that take a percentage split usually have more educational benefits for their agents. There are also brokerages that give stock options and revenue sharing plans. The education piece for new agents can be very beneficial and may warrant the commission split. Agents who have been in the business awhile and have an established client base, typically find themselves moving to a 100% brokerage at some point. Other seasoned agents choose to work for a brokerage that offers stock options and revenue sharing because they want an exit strategy. Each year, as you become more established, you should try to increase your goals by between 10% and 20%. **Your goals will help you stay on the road map of growing your success**.

Once you have your transaction goals in place, you must come up with your plan to obtain them. How many open houses a week are you dedicated to? Are you going to door knock neighborhoods? How many networking events a month will you participate in? I have a mock schedule below that I developed for my agents on my team. I also have them fill out an activity log each week that we call an Accountability Sheet. All of the activities are recommended for success. As you begin working with more clients, your daily activities will begin to shift, however I caution you to continue doing the activities that bring you future business such as open houses. You cannot allow your current business to affect your future business!

## Personal Goals:

Personal goals are different ways you want to improve your overall life. You can add fitness and weight loss goals, a vehicle you want to purchase, a home you would like to buy, more quality time with your family, or anything else that will benefit your overall life. Vision boards with photos of your personal goals can be very helpful. Having your vision board visible daily is a constant reminder of what you would like to achieve in your life.

Your personal goals should be just as obtainable as your professional goals. If you need to lose fifty pounds, maybe your goal should be twenty-five pounds at the one year mark and the full fifty at the two year mark. In order to obtain your goal of losing twenty-five pounds, you must give yourself a roadmap on how to achieve the weight loss. How many times will you work out per week? How will you change your diet? If your goal is to buy a house, how much money will you need for your down payment and closing costs? How much money will you put aside each transaction in order to make your goal a reality?

## Spiritual Goals:

Spiritual goals do not have to be organized religion related; however, they can be. Maybe your goal is to go to church every Sunday. Maybe your spiritual goal is to meditate more or use yoga as a means to relax and have time for you. Spiritual goals are the more private goals that we set forth to keep our mind, body, and spirit aligned. I have known some people to add volunteering to their spiritual goals because spiritually, it is important to give back.

In real estate, we can get so caught up in helping our clients that we forget to take time for ourselves. It is imperative to keep a work life balance and take time for you! Whatever it is that fills your energy tank is what needs to be on your spiritual goals. You become no good to anybody if you do not replenish yourself!

There are different activities you could be doing to generate more business when nobody is at your open houses, or you do not have other activities on the books. The options below are ideas to fill your time productively and help you build your future business:

- Door knock in three different steps for new listings:
  - Just before your listing hits the market, door knock with a just listed flyer and let the neighbors know that you wanted to stop by and introduce yourself because they will be seeing you and your team at the house and you wanted them to know who you are. This is a non-invasive introduction where you also invite them to come to the open house over the first weekend.
  - After the property goes under contract, door knock all of the neighbors, keeping them informed on what is happening in their neighborhood. Your flyer should be "under contract in _____ days" Let them know when you are hoping to close by and that they will see inspectors at the house and appraisers. You wanted to make them aware so that they are not concerned with strangers at the house.
  - After the property has closed, door knock to inform them that the property has closed, and their new neighbors' names are ______ and ______. At this time, you can ask for their help. "I really need your help with something. I have had so many buyers come through the property that were serious buyers, but that property did not work for them. Do you know anybody that is considering selling? Our inventory is so low and there are so many people

wanting to move into the area. If you can think of anybody in the near future, that would really help me and my clients a lot."

- Create Social Media property posts
- Create videos to save and be able to text to clients or post on social media
- Visit closed clients to see what improvements they have made to their home. They would love to see you!
- Join some type of social group to grow your sphere
- Visit new home builders to get familiar with their agents and floor models as well as pricing

Setting your professional, personal, and spiritual goals will provide you a constant reminder of where you want to be one year, two years, and five years from now. Because you wrote them down, psychologically you become invested in your success and accountable to yourself. Your goals become a foundation of how to begin, how to sustain, and how to succeed in all aspects of your life. If you do not reach every goal, it is okay! You will have a better roadmap next year. It is imperative you do not skip this step in building your success. Write your goals out and check them throughout the year to temperature check where you are. You will get there as long as you stay on your roadmap to success!

# 4

# Building a Relationship Based Business

There are a lot of "Gurus" out there who teach online marketing and the importance of buying leads. My philosophy is a little bit different. I am certainly not going to bash their ideas. They are one hundred percent correct when it comes to the importance of online presence and marketing. I have never personally paid for leads because honestly, I have never had to. My philosophy is simple; "work smarter, not harder, and as inexpensively as possible."

While working for law firms, my role was to bring in clients with virtually a zero-advertising budget. We were Foreclosure Defense firms specializing in loan modifications and short sale negotiations. I had to analyze where our clients were going to come from. Sure, we could pour money into building a website and pay for pay per click advertising and SEO, however, there wasn't a budget for an online presence. The attorneys couldn't justify the expense without first seeing the profits the division would bring in. A few people in the community were aware of my involvement with negotiations and began sending me potential clients. Very quickly, two clients became ten,

ten became twenty. By the end of the first year, we had over one hundred clients in our pipeline. There was absolutely zero money spent on advertising! Our clients all came as referrals from other clients.

By the second year, short sales were on the rise. A real estate agent came to me and asked if they could start having our office consult with their short sale clients. We, of course, agreed to offer free consultations because not everybody qualified for a loan modification or a short sale. The real estate agent was pleased to find their listing count double because of our efforts to assist their clients. The real estate agent began sending us other real estate agents that needed the same service for their potential clients. I quickly realized, if I made relationships with more real estate agents, more referrals would be sent our way. My marketing dollars were spent on taking real estate agents to lunch and hosting lunch and learns for brokerages to see the value of our services. In ten years, we never had a website or paid for advertising. I was able to help over 1000 families because of my professional relationships and that was just my client! That number does not include what the teams I built did.

You cannot put a price on relationships with professional referral partners. A referral is the equivalent of being handed a bar of gold! True referrals have over a 95% close rate. You may be asking yourself what a "true" referral is? A "true" referral is a potential client that has been referred to you by somebody they know and trust. Last year, an estate attorney called me to give me the information for a potential client. She was also helping with an estate for a deceased family member. The family lived in a northern state and needed to sell their deceased brother's home in our state. The attorney explained my services to them, obtained their permission to have me call them, and immediately called me with their information and background. I in turn, called the potential client immediately, reiterated my services, came up with a game plan for selling the home, and sent the listing agreement to be signed. I then contacted the referring attorney to let her know that we connected and were moving forward. I thanked her for her referral! From the point of contact to the close, the property and everything left in it was off their plate with money in their hands in eight weeks. The referring attorney was kept apprised of the transaction through to the end. This is a perfect example of a "true" referral and a professional referral partner.

The question you should be asking yourself right now is how to build your professional and personal referral network? Referrals handed to you are better and smarter than any paid advertising you could purchase. The simplest answer is building lasting referral relationships. As a licensed real estate professional, you cannot offer monetary compensation for referrals given to you. There is not a loophole or any legal way around this law! What you can offer is referrals in return to your professional network and exemplary customer service to your personal network. You can also drop off thank you gift for remembering you when a referral is given. Whenever a previous client sends me a referral, I immediately send them a thank you card. When their referral closes on their listing or purchase, I drop by a gift basket, thanking them again. It is important to let your previous client know how much their referrals mean to you! Why? Because it is about the continued relationship beyond the closing of their own property.

Building a professional referral network can be a little more time consuming, however can be much more fruitful. My first year in Real Estate in Arizona, I knew I needed a professional network. I wanted to make sure that no matter what services my clients needed, I knew a professional to refer them to. I created a list of every service I knew my clients might need from attorneys to a handyman, to a plumber, to a local gym. I began calling each professional and setting a brief appointment to stop by their office and meet with them. My conversations when meeting with them never began with how they could help me. My concern was making sure they were professional to refer my clients to. Setting the appointment was the first hurdle. I had to overcome their concern that I wanted something from them. Follow my example of my initial phone conversation: "Hello Mr. Smith. I am so thankful I reached you. I am a local realtor in the area and have found that many of my clients may need your services. Is there a good time for me to stop by and meet with you so that I can learn more about the services you provide?"

If the potential professional referral partner does not answer, you can leave a similar message: "Hello Mr. Smith, my name is Jane Doe, and I am a local realtor in the area. I have found that many of my clients may need your services. I would love the opportunity to stop by and introduce myself as well as learn more about the services you offer. Please call me back so that we can set up a time that is convenient for you."

You can also use the above message to formulate a similar email, however, do not get caught in the technology comfort zone! A personal phone call is much more effective. Always remember that referrals are given because of the personal touch. This fact stands true for your professional referral partners and your personal referrals.

As I was building my professional referral network in Arizona, I realized the fastest way to do so was to get plugged into a networking group. I called BNI to inquire if there were any realtor positions available. The administrator for BNI explained it would be impossible for me to get into an existing group because the realtor position always filled first. I realized I was going to have to set up my own networking group and chose a launch date. In my mind, nothing is impossible with determination and action.

I launched a "meetup" and began calling every professional I had met thus far. My first meeting had fifteen professionals in all areas of business. I was fortunate to find "core" members interested in helping me build the group. We wanted the structure of BNI, but needed to lighten up on some of the rules to meet everybody's needs. The rule we maintained and felt was the most important was one company per profession. Each member was responsible for giving referrals to other members and meeting with one to two members a week in order to build referral relationships. The networking group grew to 42 companies by the end of the first year and I netted $54,000 in real estate commissions from referrals received within the group! The results were because of the personal relationships I had built within the group. I gave many referrals to the members and because I had sent them business, they were eager to help me build my business. I never asked how they could help me. I was focused on helping them. The mindset of helping others is the key to building a successful referral network.

You may be asking yourself why I am encouraging you to build a network of professionals beyond creating referrals? One of the biggest mistakes I see with real estate agents is not having a network to refer their clients to. Let's look at the referral again that I received from the Estate Attorney. The family members did not live here and were stressed out about having to fly to Arizona to empty the home and prepare the home to be sold. Because of my network, I was able to coordinate furniture being sold, the pool being emptied, cleaned, and refilled, two vehicles being sold, all personal items being emptied out of the home and donated, landscaping being cleaned up, and the home being cleaned. All of these services were performed in three weeks with simple phone calls to professionals I trusted and had relationships with.

The point I am making is your professional referral network brings value to your clients, thus bringing value to you as their agent! As we close on a property with a client, we remind them that our relationship with them is not just through the close of their property. We want them to call us if they ever need a professional for any reason. If we do not know a professional they need, we will find one through our network. It is common for our clients to reach out to us several months after the close of their property because they need something. We are always quick to respond and help them with whatever they need. Because of our continued relationship, our clients think of us first when they hear of somebody needing a real estate agent, or if they, themselves, need our assistance buying or selling another home.

Building your professional referral network should be at the top of your list in building your relationship-based business. Referrals coming in have the highest close rate over any other marketing you can do and yet are also the least expensive. Yes, it takes time to build continued relationships but can also explode your business with phone calls coming to you. Every relationship you build both professionally and personally is potentially worth thousands of dollars in your pocket. Social media marketing and other web-based marketing and advertising will build your brand but will not carry the same closing ratios that referrals will. I have created exercises for you to help you get started or continuing to grow your professional referral networks. Always remember; it is not what they can do for you, rather what you can do for them that will make your phone ring.

Exercises:

1. Make a list of ten services your clients may need above the scope of general real estate. I have started the list for you.

| | |
|---|---|
| Landscaper | ____________ |
| Cleaning service | ____________ |
| Estate Attorney | ____________ |
| Licensed Contractor | ____________ |
| ____________ | ____________ |

2. Find five professionals that offer the services your clients may need in each category. Write down all of their contact information and call them using the scripts I have provided. Your goal is to find three per profession.

3. Set an appointment with at least three a week to understand the services they offer better.

4. Continue the relationship with follow-up emails at least once a month checking in.

5. Join a networking group or start one of your own to meet more professionals that are driven, such as yourself.

# 5

# The Psychology of the Client

We all have a fear of being "sold" and our potential clients are no different. Think of how you feel when you walk on to a car lot looking to purchase a vehicle. I don't know about you, but I get a pit in my stomach when I park my vehicle and see the salespeople lurking, waiting with anticipation to pounce. The initial reaction of most people in situations such as this is to say they are just looking. Car salespeople are taught to be persistent and pushy, which makes most people run away. We as realtors are unfortunately looked at the same way! How do we set ourselves apart and encourage potential clients to open up to us without feeling like we are being high pressure?

You will learn psychological techniques in this chapter that will not only help you in sales, but will also help you in everyday life. There is power in the ability to ease others, which opens a gateway for persuasion. The key to opening others' minds is to be like them. People like doing business with people that are like themselves. As salespeople, it is imperative to learn how to be a chameleon in regards to your personality. You will learn how to determine a potential client's personality in the first 30 seconds you meet them and will understand the words to avoid and words to use that speak to their mind and soul.

## Mirroring and Matching

The first and easiest technique to learn is mirroring and matching. Learning how to match one's speed of speech and inflection of voice will automatically help them to drop their guard. If somebody walks into your open house and is slow paced and quieter and you are fast paced and loudly excited, your potential client will freeze up and want to get away from you as quickly as possible. The same is true if somebody walks into your open house and is fast paced and excited or direct and you are slow paced and monotone.

Years ago, I was in a relationship with a man that sold cell phones for a large corporation. His sales were down greatly, and he was beginning to fear losing his job. He was never a believer in mirroring and matching or personality profiling, however, he began asking me questions. After hours of conversation and combating me on my techniques, he agreed to give it a whirl at work the next day. My questions to him were, "What do you have to lose? What do you have to gain?"

I waited with anticipation for him to arrive home and share with me how his day went with the techniques I taught him. He burst in the door excited but also with disbelief in his eyes. He had a record day in sales because of mirroring and matching. He said a gentleman walked into the store very upset. My significant other's response was the same excitement behind his questions and agreement the gentleman had a bad experience. After going back and forth with the same tone and inflection, the customer felt understood by his salesperson and felt they were alike in personality. The customer calmed down and asked if he could be helped. The customer walked away with five new phones and over a thousand dollars in accessories. More importantly, he walked away feeling helped. My significant other continued to use the Mirroring and Matching techniques and became number one in sales for the South-East Region for years in his organization. He became a true believer and began teaching others in the organization the techniques he had learned and mastered.

Body language can also be used in mirroring and matching. I do not realize I am utilizing this technique because it has become second nature to me. When anybody is sitting across from me, if their legs are crossed, mine are crossed. If they are leaning in, I am leaning in. If they are sitting back in their seat, I am sitting back in my seat. Again, people like doing business with people that are like themselves.

When I am speaking to a potential client and their arms are folded, they are closed off to the conversation. The best way to get them to unfold their arms is to fold yours in the same manner, but subtly. If you want a potential client to open up and be more interested in what you have to say, lean in as if getting ready to share a secret with them. They will automatically uncross their legs or unfold their arms and lean in as well.

Once you master the technique of Mirroring and Matching, you can then master the ability to change the outcome through your potential clients, also Mirroring and Matching you without realizing it.

## Personality Profiling

Personality Profiling is an advanced technique and one that should be practiced in everyday life. There are several books written and methods to determine the personality of potential clients. I chose what I believe to be the easiest to remember and fastest method to use in the sales field. Chase Woodford wrote the book, "Understanding Social Styles; What They are and Why They Matter." I have made the chart simple below to help make it easier to understand, however the basics are the same principles as Mr. Woodford wrote about in his book.

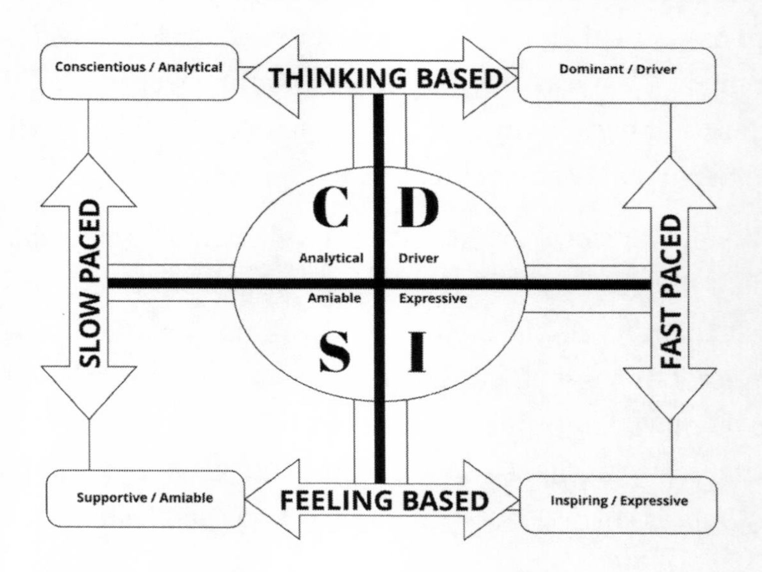

Mirroring and Matching coupled with Personality Profiling is a winning combination for success in sales. The chart below has "Thinking Based" at the top and "Feeling Based" on the bottom. It also has "Slow Paced" on the left and "Fast Paced" on the right. If one is Slow Paced and Thinking Based, their personality is more of an Analytical. If they are Fast Paced and Thinking Based, they identify as a Driver. If they are Slow Paced and Feeling Based, they are an Amiable. If they are Fast Paced and Feeling Based, they are an Expressive. Let's put this more into perspective for each personality type:

**Analytical** – A client walks into your open house and they are Slow Paced and look to the side or up prior to greeting you or answering your questions. You identify that they are Analytical. You Mirror and Match their tone and pace of speech. You follow your sales steps through slow paced, concise conversation. The Analytical will explain to you the research they have conducted to determine what they want. They will have questions for you because Analyticals always do. They pay attention to detail and will occasionally test your knowledge to determine if you are knowledgeable and trustworthy to work with. It is imperative to be clear and concise with your answers while also keeping a slow pace. You must also be careful about the answers you give because they will be checking to see if you are correct through more research if they do not already know the answer officially.

**Cautions with an Analytical** – There are cautions with all personalities and with the Analytical it is misinformation or too much information. You must also be very mindful to not use pressure techniques. The Analytical will shut down and your conversation will be over. Analyticals are the personality that will use the phrase "I need to think about this more." They will also use the phrase "I need to conduct more research prior to making a decision." If you give them too much information that they did not ask for, you will usually receive these responses. Always remember that with an Analytical, less is more, and "feelings" do not speak to them. Facts are their common language of understanding.

**Driver** – When speaking to a potential client and they are Fast Paced and Thinking Based, you have a Driver on your hands. Drivers are typically decision makers. They are typically accomplished individuals who pride themselves on who they are and what they know. They expect knowledge and expertise. The Driver will also test your knowledge to determine if you are worthy to conduct business with. After all, they are important, and their time is valuable.

**Cautions with a Driver** – Driver's do not appreciate wasting time. You must respect their time and you must never be late. They may be late, but believe that should be okay with you because of their importance. Drivers are usually uninterested in anything having to do with you. The worst thing you can do is talk about yourself or your feelings, as well as avoiding any drama. Drivers do not like being told what to do or how to do it. "Take Aways" are very effective with Driver personalities because the "Take Away" allows the Driver to feel in control even though you are the one directing. You will read more about the "Takeaway" in "Closing Sequences" later in this book. Drivers are thinking based just like Analyticals, therefore feeling based questions are like a foreign language to them.

**Expressive** – Expressives are the funniest clients you will have. They are Fast Paced and Feeling Based. They wear their expressiveness in their clothes with bright colors and patterns. They take pride in how they look and appearance matters. Expressives are typically excited about life and always looking for a party or people to be around. They are quick to make decisions as long as what they are deciding fits into their image and lifestyle. It is imperative for them to feel liked and understood. Mirroring their excitement and matching their enthusiasm is the way to their heart. They are Feeling Based so getting them emotionally involved in their decision making is a sure way to close them on an idea. Expressives hate being told they cannot have something they want, therefore the "Takeaway" is the greatest way to bring them to a yes.

**Cautions with an Expressive** – Expressives are more feeling based. They love talking about themselves, therefore keeping them on task can be a challenge. When directing them back to the task at hand, you must use caution in avoiding making them feel like you don't care about them or their life. Expressives can take twice as long to look at properties because of their fast-paced chatter unrelated to the homes themselves.

Expressives are typically late and need to understand timeframes and schedules upfront. When meeting them for an appointment, you must set the expectation that you have allotted a specific amount of time to spend with them. If you are Slow Paced, they will become bored and uninterested in you. You must keep your excitement level high with the Expressive to keep them in the game. Avoid thinking based questions and keep them emotionally involved. Speak their language of fun, friendship, and popularity.

**Amiable** – Amiables are Slow Paced and Feeling Based. They dislike being pressured and must feel a sense of friendship. Amiables do not like conflict and will fight or run when backed into a corner. They typically are very close to friends and family and are scared to death of making a wrong decision. They typically know many people and can become one of your largest referral sources as long as they believe you care about them. Amiables are longiterm clients because they are very loyal. It is not uncommon for an Amiable to want to have dinner with you instead of receiving a closing gift. Because they are feeling based, thinking based questions do not resonate with them and may push them away because of being overwhelmed.

**Cautions with an Amiable** – Amiables are relationship based. If they feel at any time you do not have their best interest at heart, they will shut down and never return your phone calls. Amiables typically need to see a home of interest several times with several different people giving opinions prior to making their own decision. They are slow paced and if they feel rushed, they will also shut down. Amiables have the kindest heart of all personality types and understanding they are typically fragile is key. Confirming their feelings and pulling them back from making poor decisions will earn you a friend and a client for life.

Understanding personalities and learning to speak their specific languages is the key to a successful sales experience. Utilizing Mirroring and Matching through tonality and pace of speech will open the door to further communication, while speaking your potential client's specific language of understanding will solidify a lasting relationship. Although the techniques taught here will feel unnatural at first, practicing in everyday life will solidify your ability to relate to others more easily. Eventually, you will become a chameleon and will be relatable to all people from every walk of life. You will learn how to be you while also matching the personalities of those around you. As you learn to master the techniques of Mirroring and Matching and Personality Profiling, you will build deeper levels of communication and understanding. The techniques will spill over into your personal relationships as well. Those around you will feel a deeper sense of acceptance from you as you begin to understand people and their actions more clearly.

The techniques taught in this chapter are the foundation of being able to understand and perform the 16 Steps for Real Estate Sales Success. Once implemented, your process will flow more naturally as you are able to meet people where they are and understand the language that speaks to their soul. The 16 Steps were created for the flow of the sales process.

The foundation laid in this chapter will help you not only grow your business, but grow it exponentially. Always remember, "People like doing business with people that are like themselves."

# 6

# Why Open Houses

In a day and age where technology seems to be taking over, people are missing the personal touch. The biggest question I hear from other real estate agents is how to meet more potential clients. For years, agents and team leaders have been paying for leads through Zillow and other sources. The conversion rates on purchased leads is less than 5%. Leads can be very costly and with the conversion rate being so low, there has to be another way! Especially for the newly licensed agent that needs to make money before they can spend money.

Real Estate is a popularity contest. The goal is to meet as many people as possible each day to fill your database. Keller Williams teaches Ignite for their beginner agents. In their program, they want you to meet ten new people, send ten thank you notes, and enter ten people into your database each day. Their philosophy is to keep getting in front of as many people as possible so that your sphere, or network, grows. When I taught Ignite, the agent's eyes would gloss over as they tried to think of ways to accomplish their goal. I would watch them until I felt their panic and then swooped in with an answer to their dilemma. I explained a very simple yet effective solution; hold as many open houses per week as possible! Not only are you showing sellers you are working at selling their property, but you are also meeting potential clients to add to your database and hopefully sell more homes to.

The next question was always the same; "how do we hold open houses if we do not have listings?" Again, the answer is simple; look at the listings of other agents in your brokerage and ask if you can hold an open house for them. All state rules are different. In Florida, we could hold open houses for any agent from any brokerage. In Arizona, we can only conduct open houses for agents that are in the same brokerage. Finding out your state's rules on open houses should be a big determining factor in which brokerage to join. Because of the rules in Arizona, I had to choose a brokerage that listed more homes in the area I wanted to work in, or "farm". I interviewed six brokerages that seemed dominant in the area and then chose the best fit for my team and I as far as fees and support. If you happen to be in a state like Florida where it doesn't matter, then choose the brokerage with the most support.

Sitting at open houses can feel a little boring if you don't know what you are doing. There are limiting beliefs out there that open houses are a waste of time. Agents believe you never sell the home you are sitting in and nobody walking in the door is looking for an agent. My team and I are walking, living proof that open houses work if you know how to conduct them properly. My first year in Arizona, I didn't know anybody other than my family. None of them were looking to buy or sell a home.

My second week with my license active, I began conducting open houses for other agents in the area. My first weekend, I received at least five leads with a commitment for continued contact. My second week holding the same home open, I sold the home to a cash buyer that walked into the open house. I was so new to Arizona Real Estate that I didn't know how to use the contract management program to write the offer so I hand wrote it! At the office, everybody wanted to know how I sold the open house. This was perplexing to me because their limiting belief did not exist in my world.

After my first success story with open houses, I began holding open houses at least four days a week. If I didn't get my ten contacts for the day in, I had to find the remaining number of contacts in different ways. It was much easier to hold open houses than cold calling for sale by owners or expired listings. My first year I closed 42 homes with over 90% of my leads coming from open houses. I began recruiting other agents and built a team on the same foundation of open houses. My team won four awards for units sold the first year! We have continued our open house platform every year and continue to exceed other teams' numbers. So much so that team leaders are coming to me wanting to learn how to conduct open houses more effectively. Many of them have expressed they are buying leads, and it is not working for them as well as it used to. They have found that it is time for them to get back to the basics.

The question you need to ask yourself is would you rather meet warm bodies with a higher potential to work with or would you rather cold call potential leads? If your answer is working with warm bodies, you must learn the techniques to be effective in bringing potential client's task tension down for them to open up to you. The 16 steps to the sales process lead you down a path of successfully converting the people that walk into your open houses into actual clients. Chapter Eleven is how to overcome objections and closing sequences. You must first master the 16 steps and then you must master overcoming objections and closing sequences.

I have included my open house protocol below, which gives you a list of items you need to set up your open house effectively. The other, most important investment is your open house signage. You must check sign ordinances for the areas you want to work in. Every city in every state is different. For instance, Scottsdale Arizona has a maximum of four open house sign rule. Our farm area doesn't have a sign ordinance within the same county as Scottsdale. I started with ten signs as a single agent but now have 300+ signs for my team. We put out 20 to 25 directional signs per open house and all are branded to my team and brokerage! Your signs should be branded to you and the brokerage you work for. The more signs you are able to put out, the more free brand recognition you will receive. Remember, this is a popularity contest so the more people that see your name, the more people will recognize you and how hard you work.

My team conducts a weekly open house tour where we have several homes open in one area. When I started out, I didn't have the luxury of a team, so I called all of the other agents with listings, from all brokerages in the area I was conducting an open house, to ask if they were planning on having their listings open as well. Basically, I created my own tour with other local realtors where we could all bounce potential buyers back and forth. I also viewed each home that was going to be open so that I knew the differences in the homes and how to sell them. This method not only helped me sell more homes, but also helped me create relationships with other local realtors.

## Dare to Be Different

Open houses bring several types of leads to your pipeline. The name of the game in Real Estate is building a bountiful pipeline in order to build your future business. Occasionally you will have the buyer that wants to buy the open house you are holding open. When this occurs, you should not hesitate and should write the offer while you are with them! Most of the time, you will have two types of leads: Those that are ready to buy or sell now and those that are wanting to buy or sell in the future. The question is, how can we be different to ensure they choose us as their agent? First, it begins with your mindset. Secondly, it is followed by your technique.

## Your Mindset:

You must keep a positive mindset when sitting in open houses. Your goal is twofold. Your first goal is to sell the house you are holding open. Your second goals are to build your pipeline of clients. Every person that walks into your open house is a potential client. They typically would not be going to open houses if they were not interested in moving at some point! It doesn't matter what they say when they walk in! They are there for a reason and it is up to you to build rapport and get them to open up to you. There is an open house protocol below that I teach for a reason. Your steps to follow are psychological and in place to bring the potential client to the point of opening up to you. You will read more about the techniques I require my team to use in steps one through five of the sixteen steps.

Most people you meet at an open house fall into two categories. Each category is just as important as the other. The first category of guest is the ones that are ready to be added to your current business pipeline, meaning they are ready to buy or sell now. The second category are the ones that are not quite ready but will be down the road. I call them my future business pipeline. Whether they are current pipeline or future pipeline, you must follow up and set yourself apart from other agents they will meet. Most real estate agents are lazy. You are not and this is where you will shine!

Whether your leads are ready now or in the future, you must exude that you are on it all the time! You must walk in confidence knowing that you are the best there is and will take care of them like nobody else. It is just as much a privilege for your leads to work with you as it is for you to work with them. Show them who you are by being different from everybody else they meet. You were created for greatness, right here, right now!

## The Ready to Buy Now Client

Once you uncover that they are ready to buy now, you must conduct your discovery thoroughly. (See discovery, step six in your steps to the sale). You must then find out their schedule for the week. What days would they like to look at homes with you? You will let them know that you are setting up a search for them but are also going to **hand choose** properties you feel meet their criteria. It is good to explain that this step is what makes you different from other agents. You do not want them getting a bunch of properties on a search that they must sift through. That is why they have you! Set your time to go look at properties with them.

## The Ready to Buy in the Future Client

We have many visitors that have already gathered their information and know they want to move into the area. Maybe they have a house to sell in another state? Maybe they have a house to sell here, and they haven't told you about it yet? Whatever their reason, it is up to you to uncover why they are waiting and what time frame they are hoping to achieve. When our guests are looking to move in the future, we need to be the ones they turn to when they are ready. How do we ensure we are at the top of their mind? By conducting discovery, finding out what they want, and setting up a search once or twice a week to begin their education to keep them updated on the market. You then need to stay in contact with them every month or so until they are ready. A Customer Relationship Management system, otherwise known as a CRM, is great but there is nothing like the personal touch! Do not be afraid to pick up the phone and call them or text them. Don't always make it about real estate either! Find personal ways to connect with your future buying clients. They will appreciate that you are not always about business and are human.

## The Wanting to List Now Client

A lot of times we have people come to an open house because they are secretly interviewing agents to list their home. They see all of your signs everywhere and they are curious why you seem so familiar to them. There is a reason all of your open houses should be set up the same and you have step to follow with every guest that walks in the door. Consistency and professionalism are what potential listing clients are looking for! They want to know that you work hard and will put your best foot forward selling their home. You must ask for the appointment to give them a value on their home. This should be explained as a no obligation, courtesy market analysis. Remember, if they walk away and you don't get the appointment, somebody else will!

## The Wanting to List in the Future Client

Occasionally, it comes out that your guest may want to sell their home in the future. You must first find out why they are waiting. If their reason is because there are more buyers during a different time frame, you must educate them on the types of buyers and the plentitude we have now. After explaining the truth about your market, they may still want to wait. That is completely okay. You can either set an appointment to give them a value now, or you can plan to touch base with them at a certain time and date.

I have a future client that will want to sell his home at some point. He has prostate cancer and is a bit overwhelmed with treatment options. When I first met him, he thought he was ready to list the property in the very near future. I visited with him for a while as he explained all that he is going through. His main objective was to make things easy on himself, however moving and not knowing where he was going to move to didn't end up being that easy for him. He was afraid to tell me that he changed his mind for the moment because he did not want to lose me as a friend. Always remember that your now and future clients all want the same thing. They want to be treated as people and not as a dollar sign. I text and call my future client just to check in on how he is feeling, never asking about real estate. I know that he will contact me about listing the home when he is ready and not concerned about his health any longer.

## Protocols for Open Houses:

Whether you are conducting an open house on your own listing or holding a listing open for another agent, there are standards that must be maintained and expectations that must be met. Your professionalism and how you conduct yourself sets you apart from other Real Estate Professionals in the market today.

## Statistics:

According to NAR in 2020, 91% of home buyers attend an open house; 52% are unrepresented and ready to hire the first agent they connect with or feel that they can trust; 9% of attendees are real estate investors or interested in investing. Open house attendees have often moved past the "research phase" and are now in the "preview phase" and are usually ready to buy or sell within 12 weeks.

Think about these statistics! If you know that you are going to be conducting an open house and 52% of the people are unrepresented, why would you not be excited about that possibility? That means that over half of the people that walk-in have not found their Realtor yet! Keep the mindset at open houses that they have been waiting to meet you!

## Before Your Open House:

Your mindset will play a bigger part of your success than anything I can teach you. Take the time before an open house to get your head straight. Make sure you are fed and rested. Be excited about what you do for a living! Always remember: People do business with people that are busy because busy = success. People like doing business with people that are like themselves because it means you understand them! Look in the mirror and tell yourself "People like me because I like people! I am successful because I make a difference in people's lives."

## Objective:

Your main objective of an open house is to sell the home you are holding open! You should never go into an open house only looking for potential buyers or sellers, although this is a huge benefit to conducting open houses. Other real estate professionals will tell you it is very rare to sell a home at the open house. DO NOT LISTEN TO THEM! I have found they are very incorrect! If the sixteen steps are followed correctly, your sales techniques and follow-up are what will give you the extra edge you need to not only sell the home at the open house, but also to attract more clients to buy or sell their homes.

## Preparation:

Each week, you should conduct at least two open houses. Whether you have a listing or have coordinated with another agent to conduct their open house and your schedule is set, go through the checklist below to ensure you are ready for success:

- Order your marketing materials (Digital flyers for social media, flyers, and door hangers)
- Proof your materials as soon as you receive the proof email and set your pickup time for the materials to be complete
- Time Block your door knocking for the neighborhood
- Look up the home on MLS and print the MLS sheet
- Create a CMA so that you know the true value of the home
- Learn the price per square foot of your open house and your list of available homes in the area
- View the photos of the other homes in the area the week of the open house so that you can speak intelligently about your competition. (You may also end up with a buyer for one of them)
- Print a list of available homes in the area for prospective buyers
- Post dates and times on MLS or ask the listing agent to do so
- Post Digital Flyers online to Craigslist, Backpage, Facebook

- Check for Chairs, Table, Water is on, AC works, Alarm Code, Pet Smells (if the house smells make sure you have candles)
- Always have a table and four chairs in your vehicle in case you need them

## The Day of Your Open House:

### Signs:

More is better! If you are placing your own signs, you will be responsible for purchasing open house signs and should have at least 15 open house signs placed per open house. The most important location is the first turn into the neighborhood off a major street. Spacing is important, giving vehicles enough time to decide if they want to turn. Not enough spacing and they will continue driving! Three open house directional signs leading up to a major intersection turn is recommended.

### Materials:

You are responsible for your materials to make your open house successful! You should have an open house box or bag that has the following:

- Laptop or tablet
- Display case for your Flyers and business cards
- Plenty of business cards
- Flyers
- Client Surveys

- Clip boards
- Pens
- Candles/Plug-in Air fresheners
- Water
- An easy snack for you to keep your energy up

**Set up of the house:**

- Get to the open house 15 minutes early **after** you have placed your signs in the neighborhood
- Place **your** open house signs in the yard with flags to attract potential clients
- Place a "come in sign" on the front door
- Turn on all the lights
- Light candles/plug in air fresheners (not too strong or flower scented)
- Turn air conditioner or heater to a comfortable setting
- Set up your table, chairs, laptop or tablet, flyers, clip boards with surveys, and pens

**During the open house:**

- Greet everybody who walks in the door
- DO NOT bombard them with questions. Be friendly and upbeat, not aggressive!
- Tell them the story of the home (the story sells a home and brings down task tension)

- Hand them a clip board and ask them to fill out your survey while walking through the home. "The sellers would really like your feedback on the home."
- NEVER follow them around the home! Let them walk around with the clip board and come to you when finished.
- Fill out the back of your survey after the potential client leaves with notes to enter into your CRM.

**Questions you can ask them when they return with the clipboard:**

- Did you find us on Zillow or was it all the signs we put out?
- Are you neighbors?
- Once complete with survey: What would you change about the home if you lived here?
- What are your favorite features of the home?
- Would it be beneficial for you as a homeowner in the area to be able to stay on top of what's happening with the values in your neighborhood?

**Follow up:**

- Send a handwritten card, use the back of the sign in sheet for your notes to make it more personal
- Email or text a link to the property, ask them to forward the email to anyone they know looking to buy
- Use CRM, enter notes and be consistent

Most leads are converted after 8-10 contacts, don't get discouraged and give up after only a few attempts. No now does not mean no forever! I have converted many open house leads by simply being the agent that never stopped working for their business. Some agents prefer to only reach out to the strongest leads. You are not MOST Agents! Reach out to everybody you meet! I encourage my team to send out 30 second videos via text thank their guests for coming in. People respond well to videos.

## Important Tips:

1. When they come to the home, don't try to convert them as a client right away. Work your sixteen steps and try to sell the home you are holding the open house on first! They will see you as a professional and you won't come off as desperate for their business. Nobody likes commission breath. This is especially important if the person you are talking to is a potential seller and you owe it to the homeowner to make that your first priority.

2. Take the time to really know the neighborhood and what has sold recently. You may take the time to preview a few of the neighboring homes on the market to compare with the one you are sitting open. If you can

answer specific questions without fumbling through papers, you will earn their trust faster.

3. Do something at the open house to stand out as they will likely meet 5 to 6 other agents that day and will be put on 5 or 6 auto drips. A great example I recently heard about was an agent that hired a magician and balloon animal maker, she killed it at the open house with 107 attendees and 7 offers in 4 hours. It does not have to be this extreme. Find something to make a joke about in the house. If the tile is hideous, don't act like you don't see it! Point it out and tell them you know the tile will be their favorite part of the home.

4. The most important thing you can do is to take good notes when you talk to people. If you're using an iPad to get people to sign in or a registration book, you're not going to be able to do this effectively. The clipboard method is this: Bottom 1/3 of the front page is the sign in area and top 2/3 is feedback section. The survey I recommend, and the clipboard technique are explained more thoroughly in step two with an example of the survey.

5. Now that you have specific and relevant information, your follow up is going to stand out from the other 5 agents they met that day. Think about it this way, if 5 agents put them on auto-drip and send them basic,

templated emails saying, "I would love the opportunity to work with you" and you are reaching out saying, "I really appreciate you helping me with the awesome feedback on the home and I would love to help your sister Linda over here from Minneapolis" you immediately stand out amongst your competition.

6. If they say they are just a "nosy neighbor" what they really mean is they are potentially a future seller and they are interviewing you right now. Stand out, be a professional and get the job!

7. Look like a professional but try to mirror the neighborhood and area. If you want to attract high-end buyers and sellers, you need to look like someone they would hire! Dress how they dress in the area you are holding the open house. If they are retired, dress more like the retirees. If they are professionals in a high-end area, dress professionally.

8. Ask a lot of questions: "What is your favorite thing about this neighborhood?" "How long have you lived in the neighborhood?" "What's the most important thing your next home must have?" "Would you be interested in learning what your home would sell for in today's market?"

9. Before your event, and all open houses should be treated like an event, make sure there are no prescription drugs, jewelry or other valuables lying around that can be easily stolen. Anything you find, you should put away and after the event put in a pile on the kitchen counter with a note, "I found these items and put them away during your open house because they are easily taken by others. Please make sure you hide these items for your future open houses."

## Think About It:

How lucky are we that we can change our store fronts without ever owning them? We can go to almost any neighborhood, price point, style, etc. It's amazing to think about! Consistency is the key to success in anything, especially with open houses. Some are going to be terrible, and some are going to rock it. You must decide that every open house is a learning experience and an amazing opportunity to grow your business! It only takes one good lead to make the open house a success! That is a lead you didn't have before conducting your open house!

You are now ready to learn the sixteen steps of the sales process from the beginning of your open house to a successful closing. Open houses are one of the best and most affordable ways to get your name out there and meet more potential clients. Learning how to collaborate with other agents in your area and creating open house tours to bring more potential buyers in will set you apart from your competition and help you to create lasting professional relationships with your peers. When done correctly, the traffic you bring into your open houses will build your current pipeline and your future pipeline of clients. The sixteen steps will take your career to a whole new level because you will understand the psychology behind everything you do. Your closing ratios will continue to rise as well as your paychecks as you learn and utilize the sales techniques you are about to embark on. With your newly learned open house skills and sales techniques, you will be unstoppable!

# 7

# The 16 Steps to the Sales Process

Many real estate agents ask me why I felt the need to put the sales process into steps. This question proves that most real estate agents do not have formal training in sales. Large sales corporations across the globe have a step by step sales process to teach their salespeople how to sell their products and services. Large corporations pay millions of dollars to develop their sales process and hire trainers to teach their salespeople. The professional sales coaches utilize a psychology behind the steps and scripts they create for each corporation.

There is a psychology behind everything we do and say in sales. Previously, you read the chapter "The Psychology of the Client." We dove into how the client sees you as a professional and the stories they create in their head prior to walking into your open house to avoid you "selling" them something they don't want. Their "task tension" is high, which means their guard is up. The sixteen steps to the sale process are designed to psychologically bring down their task tension. The steps are also designed to build trust, set expectations, build urgency, and ultimately gain commitment for future contact, leading to a closed transaction. Each step is placed for a psychological reason. Missing one of them can be detrimental to building a relationship with your potential client.

As we move through each step below, pay attention to the psychological cues. Place yourself in the position of the potential client throughout each step and evaluate what your thought process would be in their position. Steps one through five are designed to bring their task tension down. Steps six and seven are your information gathering period and confirmation to prove you were listening. These two steps build trust. Steps eight through eleven are designed to set expectations and build urgency, leading to an appointment to look at property. Steps twelve through sixteen lead your client through finding a home all the way to the close of escrow.

When following the sixteen steps, your clients will feel at ease with you. They will not feel pressure and will come to a buying decision on their own through your process. Your clients will want to refer you to others because of their positive and professional experience with you. As the agent, you will find your transactions move smoothly through the process with showing fewer homes, your clients understanding what to expect, and building their own urgency to move forward. I am excited to dive into these simple and easy yet very effective steps to the sale with you! I have also included the task tension chart to show you how you bring your potential client's task tension down and then start to build the task tension again while coming to a buying decision. Always remember, they will not open up to you if you do not bring their task tension down and they will not make a buying decision if you do not bring their task tension back up by building urgency.

## The Sixteen Steps:

1. **Meet and Greet (Personality profiling/mirror and match)**

   When a guest enters the home, greet them with a smile and thank them for coming into the open house. Ask them how they found us and make a joke about the open house signs or anything that comes to mind. Ask them permission to give the story of the home. Pay close attention before you really start speaking as to if they are slow paced or fast paced. Do they seem thinking based as you speak to them or emotionally based? Mirror and match their tonality and speed of speech. If they are speaking fast paced, you can speak fast. If they are slower paced, then take special care to speak slower to them. The key to greeting and all initial steps is your confidence when speaking. Avoid being timid or unsure at all costs! Do not enter their space and shake their hand unless they prompt it. Keep reminding yourself, how can you be different than any other agent they will meet at their open houses today.

   *Hello, thank you for coming in today. May I ask how you found us? Was it all of the open house signs that led you to me? (laugh) Well I would like to start by giving you the story of the home and then I am going to set you free, is that okay?*

2. **Story of the Home and Survey**

The story of the home should be interesting. If you do not know the story of the home, you should ask the listing agent. People identify with the property as a home if you deliver the story of the home properly. This should not be strictly features and benefits, but you can add a little of that to the story of the home to entice the guest's interest.

*The couple who owned this home loved to entertain, and the home was known as the place to be for parties at one point. The neighbors loved coming here because of the open feel in the home. Sadly, the couple had some health issues and had to move back with their family. It broke their heart to have to sell the home that they loved so much. I am sure you will see as you walk through that they poured their heart and soul into this home and maintained it well. They never thought they would have to leave.* **Go right into the survey without pause!** *It is very important to them that I receive feedback from our guests as you tour the home. They have asked me to have this survey filled out with your feedback. Please tell us what you love and what you don't, but be careful about what you don't like because I do share this with them, and I don't want to crush them (smile). Your sign in is at the bottom, if you don't want me to contact you, just let me know.* **Hand them the survey and do not hand them a flyer at this point!**

3. **Set Them Free – Let Them Come Back to You**

   Setting them free is one of the many ways we are different from other agents. You should not hover over them and create their opinions for them. This creates frustration and prevents guests from taking their time looking through the home. By setting them free, you are allowing them time to form their own opinions in their own time. You are also doing exactly what you said you would do, which builds trust.

   *Alright, you are set free to look through the home. Please let me know what you think/feel when you are finished. I would love to know your thoughts.*

   As they are walking through the home, take the a tour or open house flyer as if you forgot. Now they have seen your face twice, so by the time they come back to you with the survey, they have seen your face three times. Psychologically, it takes three times of seeing somebody before one will feel like they are friendly.

4. **Build Commonality**

   As they come back to you, they will start to open up. They may have already told you that they have an agent, or they are a neighbor that is just looking. They may tell you they are looking for renovation ideas. It is NOT the time to start breaking those walls down. Let them believe they have won in getting you off their scent of whatever story they decided before they walked in...the popcorn they want you to believe. We call it the popcorn because just like walking onto a car lot, everybody comes up with some kernel of a story to get you to leave them alone. Ask them questions about where they are originally from, do they have friends here? What made them decide to come to this area? What do they like about it? Don't ask them about the home yet. After you feel they are warm and fuzzy with you, ask them what they thought of the home. They will be more apt to be honest with you at this point. Make sure you pause and allow them to answer while you are asking them questions.

*Where are you originally from?*

*Have you been in the area for a while or are you just visiting right now?*

*So, what do you think of this home? What do you like about it? What don't you like about it?*

As they continue answering your questions, you will notice their shoulders dropping slightly and a feeling of being at ease will come over them. The more at ease they feel, the more they will open up to you. They may even sit down in your chairs at the table, especially if you are sitting down. It is very important to write everything down that they say.

5. **Break the Pact**

If you have done the previous steps correctly, you do not need to break the pact because they will break it themselves. They should feel comfortable at this point and feel like they can speak freely. They will usually tell you their real reason for coming to the open house, whether it be to find a home, interviewing agents for their listing, or maybe considering moving to the area down the road. No matter what they tell you, don't act surprised. Whatever they say, just nod your head in acceptance as if they never told you anything different. You have provided a safe place for them to just be real and open up.

*So, if I may ask, what are you looking for? You said this home is too large. Are you downsizing? Begin your discovery questions with ease. Make sure you start writing down what they say so that they can see you are listening to them. Do not interrupt them at all costs.*

6. **Discovery:**

   NEVER sell during discovery! Although it is tempting to overcome objections and questions, this is your time to gather information and build trust. The biggest mistake that any salesperson makes is selling during discovery. **If they ask you a question during discovery, let them know you will come back to that in a moment.**

   What types of questions do you ask?

   *Why the move if you don't mind me asking?*

   *When are you hoping to move by? Is there a reason why that is your timeframe?*

   *Is there another home you need to sell first? Where is it? Do you have somebody helping you with that? When are you planning on putting it on the market if it isn't already? Do you need to sell that home first prior to buying one here? Do you need anything from me regarding that property? A recommendation or referral (if out of the area)*

*Are you downsizing or upsizing? What does that look like to you?*

*When finding a home, what are the most important features you are looking for? Is the kitchen or backyard important to you? How about the bathrooms and bedrooms? Can you explain more about that to me?*

*Do you prefer warm tones or cool tones? I ask because there are some homes that are more grey tones and some with more earth tones.*

*Are you open to a home that needs a little bit or a lot of renovations to create your desired space and look? How about the yard? Are you okay with creating your desired space?*

7. **Information Confirmation:**

   Recap everything you wrote down and get confirmation that you covered everything.

   *Let me recap what I believe I hear you saying to make sure I didn't miss anything.*

   *Did I get everything that you would like for me to know? Are these the only things that are important to you or is there more? Do you have anybody helping you with your needs list?*

They are thinking of moving in a few months: *I don't know if this would interest you or not, you will have to let me know but I would be happy to set up a search for you so that you can start getting educated on the market? Does this interest you? It is really no trouble for me.....*

They are actively looking: *Are you just driving around to open houses or do you have somebody actually searching for you?* This statement creates pain that you can fix if they are just driving around. *I don't know if this would interest you, but my team has more listings than anybody in the area and we are very knowledgeable of the market in this area, I would be happy to hand choose some properties that fit your criteria and show you some of them? Would that interest you?* Notice different words I use here that are non-invasive. There is a takeaway and then I giving it back to them with pleasure. There is no way for them to feel like they are a burden and you let them know we are experts in this market. Once you get confirmation, you can move to step 8. If you do not get confirmation, keep asking questions in different ways until they end the conversation. **Never end a conversation on your own!**

They have a property they need to sell: *You had mentioned a property that you need to sell in the area, do you need a free evaluation for that property? I don't know if it interests you, but we do free evaluation with no obligation on your part. Would you like to set an appointment for me to come over and look at the property?* Notice that I use the word "property" when discussing the home they want to sell. The home they will buy is their new home! The home they are selling we need to create dissociation in their mind and that is why we call it a "property".

8. **Search:**

   Our whole strategy is how do we differentiate from every other agent they meet! One of the ways we do that is by listening to what they really want and then **hand choosing** properties for them that fit their needs, wants, and desires. Other agents just put them on a general search and basically say happy hunting, let me know if you want to see anything.

   *I am going to set up a general search for you, based on your criteria, that you will receive regularly. A couple of times a week, starting today, I am going to hand choose you properties that I feel are the best options based on your requests. These emails will be titled "Properties I hand chose for you". I will check in from time to time to make sure I am on the mark. How do you prefer me to check in with you, text or phone call?* (This is a trial close and confirmation that you they want you to contact them)

9. **Build Urgency:**

   Building urgency starts with setting an expectation by educating the potential clients on the market in their area. Remember, don't assume they live in the area or know anything about it. It is up to you to educate them so that they do not get disheartened while looking when they find what they want. It also builds a desire to find something before there is nothing left.

***Now,*** *if you find something you believe you may be interested in, it is very important we go see it right away! Out of 17,000 homes in this area, there are only 166 total on the market. Properties are not staying on the market long because of the low inventory and I don't want you to miss out because we have waited too long. Yes, occasionally we are in multiple offer situations. I am very equipped to handle these types of situations. When do you think you will want to start looking?* (this is your trial close in this section)

10. **Follow up:**

    Do not wait to set up their search! You must do exactly what you said you will do, or you will create mistrust! Get it done the day you say you are going to. Set up their general search and then set up their first set of hand chosen properties in a separate email that day. The biggest failure of agents is not doing what they say they are going to do! Do not fall into that trap and habit. You will miss several opportunities. Follow up with them the next day to make sure they received it and ask what they thought of the properties you found.

    *Would you like to set up a time to go view a couple of the properties I chose for you? Do you feel I captured what you are looking for? Did you see any others that you might like to see as well in the general search I sent you?* (This is a closing question)

11. **Set Appointment**

When setting an appointment to view properties, give them different time frames you are available on two different days. Ask if any of the time frames work for their schedule. Psychologically, by giving time frames, it plants the seed that you are a busy professional. **People like doing business with professionals that are busy.** This technique also trains them that you are not just available all the time, so they will need to honor their appointments as well as schedule in advance.

*I am excited you found a few homes you would like to see! I have today between three and five available or tomorrow between ten and twelve. Do either of those times work for you? No? Okay, what is the best time for you, and I can see if I can move some things around in my schedule.*

12. **Showing Property – The Viewing Experience**

The day of the appointment, be prepared with everything you need. Your promptness is very important. Make sure all of your showings are set up with confirmation from the listing agents. Make sure that you let your client know how much time you believe it will take to view the properties they would like to see.

Listen to their thoughts while viewing a property. Agree with them when appropriate. Shaking your head yes a lot as you speak (psychological), and notice that they start shaking their head yes more and more. Take notes on each property. You should have a property information sheet for them and for you. You should also have an extra pen with a clip board for them so that you can both make notes on each property.

If they are from out of town and you are comfortable, drive them in your vehicle and have a small cooler of water for them. Make sure you take them on a tour of the area and explain the features and benefits of the community they want to live in. Use some of what you found out in discovery during this part of your viewing experience! It is good for you to point out things they told you were important to them. It shows that you still remember and took their needs to heart. It also shows that you care about what is important to them and are looking out for them. It is okay for you to point out things they said they wouldn't like. This also continues to build trust and shows them you want their happiness and their needs met. You are not in it for a paycheck, you are in it for them and will protect them. At the end of each viewing experience, do a temperature check.

*Overall, how do you feel about this property? What did you like and not like? Do you believe it checks most or all of your boxes of needs? What could make it a better property for you? We have a couple more properties on the list so let's make notes on this one and if we need to circle back to any of them, please just let me know.*

If they do not like the property: *Ok so this property is definitely a no? Go ahead and give me your sheet so that we do not confuse it with other homes you do like.* Take the sheet and rip it in half in front of them. This is a "takeaway" and something you will learn more about in overcoming objections and closing sequences. They will think twice before telling you a home is a no moving forward.

13. **Close**

When you have walked into the property that seems to be the right fit for your clients, confirm features and benefits based on their discovery and other properties you have seen. Compare the property with properties they didn't seem to like. *So, what do you guys think? Is this the one? Are we prepared to make an offer?* (Closing question)

If the answer is yes, discuss what their thoughts are on making the offer as far as amount. If they have no idea, make a suggestion and wait for their response. Write the contract! Don't talk too much during this time. If they are ready, start the process immediately. You should AWLAYS have contracts and supporting documents printed in your vehicle. There is something magical about them taking the pen and signing their name. It makes it more real.

If their answer is no, not yet, ask them what the hesitation is on this one. Acknowledge that it may not be the right property if they are not completely feeling it. Continue looking at any new properties you see, and compare to this particular property. They may change their mind on this one after seeing some of the others. Don't push, just gently nudge when needed.

14. **Contract written**:

    Be prepared with everything you need for the property they want to write an offer on. It is always a good idea to have printed contracts with you just in case they want to write an offer at the property. They may want you to email them the contract and electronically sign as well. Setting the expectation of what happens next is the key to your success in writing the contract and moving forward through the purchase of the property. Remember, we do this every day, they do not! Our language of real estate is a daily ritual for us. For them, it is a foreign language. Be sensitive to this as you are going through the contracts with them. During this time, you also need to set expectations to prevent your clients from being caught off guard by any outcomes.

    Low offers: *The seller may want to counter your offer, so it is important you have an idea of what you are really willing to pay for this property. After reviewing the comps in the area and knowing the price per square foot, I feel you can go as high as ___________ and not overpay for the home. What are your thoughts?*

Potential multi-offer situations: *There are many buyers and not enough properties, we should probably put our best foot forward with this home. I recommend we come in at ____________. It is important to me that you feel comfortable with your offer as well as have a great chance of getting the offer accepted. We do have a clause we can add as well so that if there are other offers, we protect you to have the right to offer more, but you are not obligated to. (Acceleration Clauses are state specific so this only applies if your state allows them) What are your thoughts?*

Once the offer is written: *I am going to call the agent to let them know we are sending the offer today. We have a deadline on the contract for them to answer us by ____________ time. If they miss the deadline and are communicative about it with me, it can always be fixed with an addendum. Sometimes sellers need to be presented with the offer in person and it may take a little longer so please do not stress out about it. I will stay in close contact with the agent and keep you updated.*

*After the offer is negotiated and agreed upon, we will want to schedule your inspection right away. We have ten days to get our requests to them, if any, on items that we want fixed. What day works best for you for the inspection? I have a transaction coordinator, (name of transaction coordinator), that takes over from the point of contract to close for all documents. They make sure all I's are dotted and all T's are crossed. I am still a part of the transaction and will be negotiating the inspection requests for you. I will also be getting updates on the appraisal amount and making sure we are on track to close on time. Your role during all of this is to check your email regularly in case my transaction coordinator needs anything from you. After the inspection and appraisal are complete, we will be doing a final walk through together prior to your closing. You will also need to get utilities in your name for the closing date. The closing is your date, everything needs to be put in your name. We have a list of those providers if you need them to make it easy for you. I am telling you all of this to make sure you know what to expect but I will also be reminding you every step of the way. It is not necessary for you to remember everything right now. Do you have any questions for me at this time before I submit the offer?*

15. **Negotiation – The Art of Negotiation Chapter**

    There are several negotiating techniques discussed in The Art of Negotiation chapter. I recommend learning them like the back of your hand.

16. **Closing of Escrow:**

    It is your responsibility to make sure your clients set up their utilities and schedule the final walk through with you. It is also suggested that you provide some type of closing gift for them. Home warranties and things that are not actually handed to your clients are not good closing gifts. Gift baskets with gift cards are always a nice gift. It is also important that you explain how the close of escrow works and when they will get their keys to move in. This differs from state to state.

*The day you close is your close of escrow. In order to receive your keys in Arizona, the closing documents must be recorded. It is usually recommended if you want your keys to move in that day that we have your signing of documents and money wired a couple of days prior to the closing date to ensure the transaction can be recorded the day of the closing in the morning. I can turn over your keys to you by early afternoon. Do you have any questions about this part of the process?*

*I will be coordinating with title for your signing. Would you like to go to the office or have a mobile notary sent to you? I will do everything I can to be there for your signing.* It is recommended that you are there for their signing in case they have any questions. This also makes them feel cared for. You can choose to bring their closing gift to the signing, or you can give it to them when you give them their keys.

After the close of escrow and delivery of keys, you should mark it on your calendar to check on your clients within five days of the closing to ensure they are happy. You should then follow up with them every three months to touch base and find out if they need anything.

The psychology of the potential client is one that needs to be understood. Throughout the sixteen steps of the sales process for buyers, you differentiate yourself from your competitors. You build rapport, trust, expectations and urgency. By following each step, you are leading your clients down a path of finding what they are looking for with ease of the process. They will treat you like the professional you are and will not be caught off guard by any situation that comes their way. You have proven to care about their needs and wants as well as become their advisor, not their sales agent! Nobody wants to be sold. Everybody desires a professional who cares about them and truly knows their field of expertise. Your clients should feel like you are their friend.

You may realize you are already utilizing some of these techniques, but didn't know why. The sixteen steps create a system that can be mimicked over and over again. If your sales begin to fall, the steps make it easy to pinpoint what you have gotten away from so that you can reset your strategy. The steps bring you to a conscious successful because you know exactly what you are doing and why!

# 8

# The 16 Steps to the Listing Process

Listing properties is one of the most important processes to understand as a licensed Real Estate agent, however they are also one of the most feared presentations. Listings are an entirely different animal than buyer's appointments because your client will have a predetermined idea as to what their property is worth. Every listing client believes their property is a castle. It doesn't matter if it is their home and they have lived there for twenty years without any improvements, or they put blood, sweat, and tears into an investment property, it is a castle. Your goal is to bring the client to reality of what their property is worth while winning the listing.

First, you must understand the psychology behind the listing client. Nine times out of ten, they are emotionally connected to the property. There is a reason they want or need to sell, but there is usually a part of them that is hesitant. Uncovering their fears, attachment, and motivation is going to be your priority prior to selling them on why you are the right choice for the job. Just like buyers, listing clients want to feel heard and understood. You must always assume your listing client is interviewing other agents, which is another reason agents fear listing appointments.

A couple of years ago, I had an agent on my team that received a referral for a listing appointment. After a few days, I followed up with her to find out the results of the call. My agent had to admit to me that she never attempted to contact the referral out of fear. I realized at that moment that we were dealing with a paralyzing fear on the side of my agent. As we spoke, she explained the referral partner told her the potential client was interviewing agents. The thought of going up against other agents and potentially losing was too scary for her, so she just let it go. As we uncovered her fears we had to deal with the fear of rejection as well as her lack of confidence in her ability to explain value. These are very real fears that most agents have. They become limiting beliefs that prevent us from success. The 16 steps to the listing process was developed to conquer those fears. I developed the listing steps specifically for my agent so that we could build her confidence. She became the top listing agent on my team because of her confidence, knowledge and limitless belief in herself!

## 16 Steps to the Listing Process:

Steps 1 through 7 of the 16 steps to the Buying Process are the same steps for the 16 Steps to the Listing Process. It all begins with open houses. Refer to the previous chapter for more detail on the first 7 steps, however I will list them here as a reminder.

1. **Meet and Greet**
2. **Story of the Home and Survey**
3. **Set them Free**
4. **Build Commonality**
5. **Breaking the Pact**
6. **Discovery**
7. **Information Confirmation**

From the point of meeting your potential client through discovery and information confirmation, you will uncover the potential client has a home to sell. In many, but not all, instances, the potential client has a home they need to sell because they want to buy another one. Your mindset must be that they are either going to hire you or somebody else, so why not you?

### Step 8. Set the Appointment for the Property Evaluation

Asking a potential client if they would like a "free and "no obligation" evaluation on their property is a non-invasive way to get in front of them. You will meet potential clients that have no idea what their home is worth and have no idea if purchasing another home is feasible. While setting the appointment, you are simply becoming an advisor.

*It sounds like you need to know what your property is worth before you can make any decisions on how you want to move forward. I don't know if this interests you or not, you will have to let me know, but I would be happy to stop by and give you a free, no obligation, evaluation of your home. Is that something that interests you? At least then you would know where you are with your current property so that you can make some educated decisions on how to move forward.*

It is especially important at this point that you stop speaking and listen to what they have to say. Your verbiage is psychologically chosen to make them feel like it is their choice even though you are directing them to allow you to evaluate the property. At this point, serious potential clients will lower their guard even more and decide there is no harm in having you stop by.

*Wonderful. Are you available Tuesday afternoon around 3:00 or would another time work better for you?*

**Step 9. Create your Market Analysis**

Prior to your appointment, you must create your comparative market analysis (CMA). It is important to utilize your MLS tools to find like properties within the actual neighborhood your potential client lives in. You should go back at least six months unless there are not many properties available to compare. You may need to go back twelve months if this is the case.

There are many programs that create elaborate CMAs with tons of information. In my opinion, simple is always better. You do not need a full report with school information or every comparable property information sheet or Plano as we call them. All you need is the comparable properties basic information, a list of pending, closed, and listed properties, and your low, medium, average and high values for your subject property. Your CMA should not be more than ten pages in most instances unless there is a lot of comparables.

You should print one copy for you and one copy for the client. While looking at the comparable properties, it is a good idea to scroll through the photos to understand why some are more than others. Usually it is because there are several upgrades or improvements. Understanding the differences will help you explain the value of your potential client's property or home. I do not recommend sending the CMA to your potential client ahead of time. They will see the values and decide what their property is worth prior to you visiting and comparing the property visually to your comparables. Remember, everybody believes they have a castle, even if the home is in its original state, compared to the home down the street that is completely renovated!

### Step 10. Property Tour, Numbers and Pricing

When meeting your clients at their property, it is imperative you are on time! If you are running even two-minutes late, or think you might be, you must call them and let them know. Always remember, a property evaluation is a job interview and the potential client is your potential employer. Always put your best foot forward and treat them as such! On the flip side, you are also interviewing them to determine if you are willing to take them as a client. I have turned down listings in the past because the potential clients were unreasonable with expectations and pricing.

As you walk up to the property, your eyes should be open to the condition of the exterior of the home. How does the roof look? Is the paint in good condition? How about the landscaping? These are key factors in pricing the home. Once your potential clients greet you and you enter the home, while standing in the foyer, ask if you should start with a tour of the property.

> *Hello Jim and Lisa, thank you for having me over. Would you like me to take off my shoes? Would it be okay if we start with a property tour? I would love for you to show me your home and what you love about it as well as anything you may not like about it.*

The client will always be happy that you asked to see the home. They will take pride in sharing anything they have done to the home. They will also share things they have not been fond of. This is important information for your toolbox when finding them a new home. You should have a notepad with you and take notes on any upgrades they mention, as well as when they were completed. You also need to know the condition of the roof, the year the hot water heater was purchased, and the condition of the air conditioning unit.

After the property tour, ask the clients if it is okay to sit at the table to discuss numbers. You want to make sure they sit across from you together so that you can see both of their faces. Their facial expressions will tell you how they are feeling as you go through numbers and will prevent hidden cues between the two of them. If they attempt to sit on each side of you, it is okay to ask them if you can seat them together so that they both can see what you are presenting. Do not be shy about this! Having a view of both of them is **imperative** for your presentation.

As you pull out your CMAs, you will confirm the information you learned from them about the property by utilizing information confirmation. You will then ask them what the plan is when they sell their property. Most agents do not realize this question is important, however it is fundamental in setting the stage that you care about their future and plans. Also, take note that I changed the word "home" to "property" in this section. You are psychologically setting the stage for them to begin letting go of the property and moving forward. The word "home" equates to ownership. The word "property" means just that, a property that can be sold.

*Jim and Lisa, you have a beautiful property. As we walked through, you shared with me x, y, and z. You also shared with me that the roof was replaced in ________, the hot water heater is ______ years old, and the air conditioning unit is original but serviced every six months and works amazingly. Did I miss anything?*

*Now, before we go over the value of the property, based on everything that has sold in your area, I need to make sure I understand your future plans. It is important to me that we do not sell your property prior to having a plan for after the sale.*

During this portion of the process, you are getting them emotionally involved in letting their current home go. By focusing on the future, they will naturally begin to detach emotionally from their current property and begin attaching to the future plan.

After the tour of the property, there is a sequence of closing and getting commitments. There are different objections and closes shown below to help guide you through different scenarios.

> *Thank you for showing me your property and having me over today. I appreciate you trusting me and taking the time for me to share this information with you. Let me show you what my comparables say and then we will go over my thoughts on what your property is worth.* ***Is that fair?*** (This is a tie down statement. You should be shaking your head yes when you ask tie down questions and they will mimic you automatically. You can read more on tie downs and other closing techniques in the Overcoming Objections and Closing Sequences chapter)

Present the numbers based on the comps, tell them your thoughts on what you are coming in at for list price.

> *(Their Name), one of the biggest things I look at in pricing your property is the amount and types of upgrades you do or do not have. Based on viewing your property (list upgrades or lack of upgrades), because of these factors, I feel your property is worth $___________.*

*This number is based on what has sold in your area in the past six months that is comparable to your property.* ***What are your thoughts/feelings based on what I have explained?*** (Shut up and listen!)

You should be watching their body language and their movement of eyes during the previous segment. If they shift in their seat, dart their eyes, look at each other with a funny look, or any other indication they are uncomfortable, it is time to be decently bold and ask them directly if the number is higher or lower than they were thinking.

**If they agree with your price opinion:**

*I'm glad we are on the same page!* (Move to the next closing questions)

**If they do not agree:**

*Ok, I hear what you are saying, what were you hoping for?* (shut up and listen)

*Why were you hoping for that number?* (shut up and listen)

Run the numbers based on square footage and determine if we can come close to what they were hoping for.

*Based on square footage, because that is how appraisers look at properties in this area, price per square foot depending on upgrades, I feel we cannot go higher than $_________. The reason is because my job is not only to get you the most money for your property, but also* *in most cases, unless it is a cash offer, I also have to make sure I can get it to appraise. You would be pretty upset if I sold our property and we couldn't get it to appraise for the offer amount,* ***wouldn't you agree?*** *(Tie down) So I say we start at $____________, test the market and see what kind of response we get. If we are not getting showing requests, then we will know we are priced too high and need to adjust in a couple of weeks.* ***Are you okay with that strategy?*** (Get commitment to move forward!)

**In a heavy seller's market**, you may also want to explain that the goal is multiple offer. Our goal is to price the property to draw people in so that they become emotionally attached to the property and are willing to bid against other offers. If we price the property too high, we may not get as much for the property as we would be pricing the property lower. We can also explain appraisal contingency waivers and how they come into play in a bidding seller's market.

**Showing the numbers broken down:**

*Let me show you a couple of different scenarios of offers so you can see what you will net, because at the end of the day, that is what matters most,* ***would you agree?*** (Tie down)

Write down an offer amount of $5,000 less than what you are listing for. Subtract 6% realtor commissions from the gross proceeds and show the total underneath. Then subtract 1% for estimated closing costs. *Do you have a loan on the property? If so, how much do you owe?* If they have a loan, subtract the estimated payoff amount from the total. Circle the bottom number and write NET next to it. Do the same math with an offer for $10,000 less than the previous Gross offer. Once you have completed both scenarios, turn the paper around and explain both to them. Examples are below:

(First Example)

| | |
|---|---|
| Listing price | $199,900 |
| Gross offer amount | $195,000 |
| Realtor commissions 6% | -$11,700 |
| | $183,300 |
| Estimated closing costs 1% | $1,950 |
| | $181,350 |
| Loan amount | $0 |
| NET | $181,350 |

(Second Example)

| | |
|---|---|
| Gross offer amount | $185,000 |
| Realtor commissions 6% | -$11,100 |
| | $173,900 |
| Estimated closing costs 1% | -$1,850 |
| | $172,050 |
| Loan amount | $0 |
| NET | $172,050 |

***In a heavy seller's market**, you would do this same exercise with asking and $10,000 higher as your second example.

> *I want you to have a good idea of the range when we receive offers.* Point to a higher offer amount and go down the list explaining each item. When you get to commissions, state it this way; *This is all realtor commissions, meaning if another agent outside of our team sells your property, they will receive 3% and we will receive 3%. The next item is the estimated closing costs, which could be a little higher or a little lower depending on prorations. So, after all expenses are paid out, this is what you will put in your pocket.* ***How do you feel/think about that number?*** (Get confirmation or you cannot proceed!!!!!)

**Hard Close**

> ***When would you like for me to get the property on the market?*** (Please note I said property and not home as to disassociate from the property)

**They are ready now or next week**

Get confirmation by repeating back to them what they said to you. *Ok, right away, let's get everything scheduled.* Move to next step.

**They are not ready, and you need to uncover the root objection:**

> *I understand you are not ready quite yet, which tells me you are having some hesitations on selling your*

*property and when. May I ask what your concerns are? This helps me to help you better.* (Shut up and listen and let them puke all over you! Do not start talking until they are done.) Handle each objection one by one, confirming their thoughts and feelings while presenting solutions. Remember, a problem is not a problem if there is a solution! After you overcome each objection one by one, you can ask them. So, *we have covered all of your concerns (list each concern again with the solution),* ***are you more comfortable now to move forward and set a date for listing the property?*** (Remember in this moment you have nothing to lose and everything to gain. If you walk out that door without a firm commitment, you will more than likely lose the listing to the next person that walks in the door. Are you willing to lose it because of fear of hearing no?) *Wonderful, I have a listing contract in my car that is blank that I can fill out?* Do not hesitate in asking this question and always make sure you have a listing agreement and all supporting documents in your vehicle so that you can strike while the iron is hot!

### Step 11. Confirm Open house Schedule, Photos, Lockbox and Sign

Once you have a commitment on pricing and your client's desire to move forward with the listing, you must finalize the commitment with confirmation on the marketing plan.

*Jim and Lisa, we need to come up with our official marketing plan for the property. What day are we hoping to have this on the market by? We recommend allowing us to hold at least two open houses a week to gain more traffic on to your property. There are no better marketers for your property than the ones that live in your neighborhood. We have great success selling properties at the open house. We prefer to conduct the open houses the day the property hits MLS. Our thought process is that we will receive so many showing requests that we may run out of times available for agents to show the property. Having the property open the first two days especially will allow everybody to see the property that they want, therefore encouraging more offers. Does Saturday and Sunday work for you the first weekend? I also need to set a time for your professional photos to be taken, sign to be installed, and the lockbox to be placed on the property for other licensed real estate agents to be able to show the property. Is there a specific time and day that works best for you? If we would like the property on the market for the weekend, it is imperative we have photos taken by Wednesday if that works for you? I am writing all of this down to leave with you as well so that we stay on the same page with dates and times.*

## Step 12. Enter Into MLS and Create Marketing Materials

Once you receive the photos back, you are ready to enter your new listing into MLS. Your property description is the most important piece in your MLS listing. You should write a description with enticing words describing the features and benefits of the property. After writing the description, email it to your clients so that they can add some flare as well. Inviting them to participate makes your clients feel they have some control. When this step is missed, your clients will inevitably call or text you that they want changes to the description. To avoid more work for yourself, why not allow them to be a part of this step from the beginning?

Your photos should always be professionally done and uploaded into MLS because your photos showcase your brand and how professionally you are for other potential listings. Giving each room a name and positioning your photos in a certain order is important as well. I prefer my photos to begin with the front of the property, move through the natural floor plan of the property and ending with the back yard. If the property is on a substantial lot size or the view is spectacular, you should spring for the drone video as well to showcase the additional features. A perfect example of needing a drone video is a property being downtown, near everything and you want to showcase how close everything is. Another perfect example is a property that has a view of a lake. The drone video will capture the essence of the tranquility of living on the lake and entice buyers that are looking for that specific lifestyle. I do not believe a drone is needed for every listing. Not all properties look amazing from an aerial view, and having a drone video done for these types of properties could have an adverse effect on your showings.

Property flyers are important but with limited information being showcased. Having a flyer box on the sign is important because potential buyers will want readily available information. I recommend one to three photos in color, the price, bedroom and bathroom count, square feet, and a list of upgrades if applicable. Nothing more than this information along with your contact information. It is also important under your contact information, in bold print, "PLEASE CALL ME FOR YOUR SHOWING APPOINTMENT."

## Step 13 Receiving Offers and Negotiating

When receiving offers, your client wants to know the bullet points of the offer and their net when all is said and done. What you need to pay close attention to is:

A. Offer Amount
B. Closing Date
C. Are the buyers requesting a property warrant?
D. Are the buyers requesting seller concessions?
E. Are they obtaining a loan, what type, and is there a prequalification letter attached?
F. Are they paying cash? If so, their proof of funds is attached.

G. Are the Washer/Dryer and/or Refrigerator included in the offer?
H. Are there any additional requests in additional notes?
I. Is there an appraisal contingency waiver?
J. Is there an acceleration clause?
K. Who is the title company on the offer?
L. Are the buyers offering anything else to your seller that is important?

You should always call the sales agent to introduce yourself and confirm receipt of their offer. In a multiple offer situation, call the agents with the highest offers. This step establishes a relationship and rapport with the sales agent. You can then ask about the buyers and if there is a story the agent would like you to share with your sellers. You are asking for the story because it makes the buyers people to your sellers and not just a number on the contract. If the buyer is obtaining a loan, it is also a good idea to call the lender and inquire whether the buyers have turned in their financial documents already and if there are any red flags you need to be aware of.

Once you have all of the information, it is time to present the offer or offers to your sellers. Call your sellers and explain the story of the buyers, your conversation with the lender, and all pertinent information regarding the offer. You must then do the math with your sellers, the same as during the listing appointment. If there are additional costs to the seller, such as seller concessions or a property warranty, make sure you subtract the amounts on your net sheet as well to ensure you are giving them as accurate an estimated net as possible. Make sure you use the word "estimated" net.

During the conversation with your sellers regarding the estimated net, it is advisable to also explain the next steps in the process being the inspection. There may be additional items that will cost money to fix if the buyer requests repairs based on the inspection. You are setting the expectation up front that this scenario could happen so that the sellers are not surprised if or when the request comes in.

If the offer you received is low, your conversation with the sales agent is that your clients are more than likely going to counter and the buyers are prepared for that. Again, you are setting expectations on both sides so that there are no surprises. **Surprises are the silent killer of all negotiations.** Please see "The Art of Negotiations" chapter for further information on this technique.

### Step 14. The Inspection

The inspection period is the number one timeframe when transactions fall out of contract. The biggest reasons are major repairs needed and buyers or sellers being unreasonable with their requests and responses. Please review "The Art of Negotiations" chapter to master maneuvering through this process.

Your sellers should be informed that there cannot be any clutter in areas the inspector needs to access such as the attic, hot water heater, and Air Conditioning areas. Nobody should be on the property while the inspector is there. It is not advised for you to be at the property while the selling agent is going over the inspection findings with the inspector and the buyers. The buyers are the customers of the inspector in most cases and the inspector should not share information with their customer if you are present.

### Step 15. The Appraisal

When the appraisal is scheduled, you, as the listing agent should always be there without fail! Your job as the listing agent is to prove the value of your listing. This is all only important if you do not have an appraisal contingency waiver! If you do have the appraisal contingency waiver, the following does not apply.

You should have the following with you to give to the appraiser:

A. Current CMA printed
B. If there were multiple offers, the first page of each additional offer printed to show how much interest there was at the listing price
C. A list of upgrades on the property and when they were completed
D. If the AC, roof, and/or hot water heater are newer when they were installed
E. Slide in the story of the property while speaking to the appraiser

Just like our buyers and sellers, we must prime the appraiser psychologically to not only see the value of the property, but to also humanize the transaction into people and not just numbers associated with a property. If the appraiser feels the human side, they will do everything in their power to make the numbers come in where they need to if the comparable properties align with the information you have provided. They will give extra effort to do so.

**Step 16. Close of Escrow**

The day your clients sign their closing documents is an emotional day for several reasons. They are closing a chapter of their life. They are leaving a property. Most clients are excited the process is over and looking forward to their next chapter. For some, the closing is emotional depending on the circumstances surrounding their need to sell. Whatever their emotional state, you must be there for support! You should have a gift in hand, ready to give them when the signing is complete. Hopefully, you are also signing documents for their purchase as well! You have been their rock and their guide throughout this process. You have become their friend and trusted advisor. It is important to show them your relationship does not end here, and you will always be a continued resource for them. Refer to the chapter "Your Client for Life" to set the expectation for continued contact.

As you can see, following the 16 Steps to the Listing Process gives you a psychological guide from the first meeting of your client all the way through to the closing of escrow. Following the steps and mastering how to price properties takes the fear on your side away because of the confidence you exude. Effectively listing properties is all about your confidence in your ability to price accurately, market the property, and negotiate offers. Once you master the steps, you will find more and more potential clients say yes to you listing their property. Very rarely will you lose to other agents because you are so confident, but not egotistical, in your abilities to sell a property. They have no choice but to believe in you because you believe in yourself!

# 9

# THE ART OF NEGOTIATION

Negotiations are the most important and sometimes toughest part of a transaction. Learning the skills of negotiating will set you apart from 62% of other realtors, however if you become a master negotiator you will rise above over 80% of your competition. Negotiations are a skill that can be learned, although some have a natural instinct to think like a negotiator.

I was fortunate to mentor under attorneys for ten years in foreclosure defense, short sale, and loan modification negotiations. I built foreclosure defense departments through setting up the lawyer's systems, designing their defenses, hiring their negotiators, training the negotiators, and bringing in all of their clients. My main role, other than bringing in clients, was to learn the lender's parameters and negotiate loans either through short sales or loan modifications. Once the parameters were understood, there were simple steps to follow to ensure a smooth negotiation where both parties win in the end.

## Step 1 - Know and understand your opponent

Having an understanding of who and what you are dealing with on the other end helps you guide your client through the negotiation. Prior to writing an offer, you should call the other realtor to accomplish several items for success:

- Introduction to you – they need to know who you are and what team and/or brokerage you are with.
- Let the agent know you are sending an offer and politely ask that they not accept another offer without first seeing yours. You should always ask if they have other offers, as well as if you need to know anything about the offers they have received.
- Tell the agent the story of your buyer. This makes your buyers people instead of numbers. This technique allows the agent to explain the buyers to their client and opens the "compassion window" with the agent and the seller.
- Finish the call with the expectation of when the offer will be received, and you will send them a text confirming you sent it.

### Step 2 - Setting Expectations

When you set expectations up front, you have left little room for surprises. Surprises are what kill transactions dead in their tracks. Throughout the fourteen steps of the sales process, you are setting expectations. From the moment you meet your prospective client all the way through to the closing process, you have set the stage of all possibilities and scenarios so that your client can be prepared for any turn of events and not be caught off guard. Imagine your client falling in love with a home. They are completely excited about their offer being accepted as it is and mentally, they start moving in. You haven't laid the foundations of what could occur and receive a rejection or a multiple counter. You present this to your client, and they become enraged! Why? Because you did not prepare them for this, and they are now feeling a potential loss. Who do they blame? You! They see you as the source of causing them pain. Setting proper expectations lessens the pain because they are not caught by surprise.

### Step 3 - Information Confirmation

After you have set expectations, it is crucial to confirm with your client that they not only understand the next step, but also, they know what to expect down the road. Information confirmation is where you solidify what has been discussed, confirm agreement and understanding, and confirm what you are preparing in the document for them to sign. Everything that you confirm should be followed up in your email as written proof of the conversations.

*Dear Sam,*

*I have prepared the counter to the offer on your property, just as we discussed. We are countering the price at $________. We are agreeing to all other terms of a 30-day close and a 10-day inspection period. We also discussed how they may counter you again. Once under contract, they will send a list of items that come up on inspection to be repaired. I will have my contractor* *give you pricing on their request. You and I will discuss what you are okay with fixing and the items you will decline. I will continue to market your property through the 10-day inspection period. Please let me know if you have any questions.*

What is the reason for backing up all information discussed in an email? Number 1, it is to cover your rear if there is ever a question down the road. Number 2, when the inspection comes later and your client potentially throws a tantrum, you can bring up this conversation and there can be no rebuttal that you talked about. Always remember, people conveniently forget when it benefits them. By confirming the conversations in writing, there is no room for convenient forgetfulness.

**Putting the Three Steps into Action**

When writing an offer with your client, you should know how many days the property has been on the market, as well as if there are other offers you are up against. It is up to you to set the expectation of potential counters and bidding wars. You should also understand the value of the home. Your conversation should be had as follows:

*"Dave and Joan, I spoke to the agent and here is what we know about the sellers and whether they have any offers on the table. The sellers are moving into an assisted living facility and are much older in years. They are having a hard time taking care of themselves because of some health problems.*

*The property has been on the market eight days and the agent said she has been told they have an offer coming in, but they have not seen it yet. I have asked them not to accept any offers until they see yours first and they have agreed to my request. I have reviewed the numbers and they are pretty on point with their asking price. What are you thinking you would like to offer? (Whatever they say you should agree to). Ok, I will write the offer for $______.*

*Now I would like to share some scenarios that could occur. The seller could counter the offer. They can decline the offer without a counter, or they can accept the offer. If they have multiple offers, they can choose to multiple counter asking for everybody's highest and best or they can just go with another offer because of terms. Do you have any questions about the different scenarios? Based on this information, are you happy with where we are submitting the offer? I will get that over via email right away so that I can submit to the agent. We probably won't hear back from them until tomorrow."*

Let's use another negotiation scenario: Your seller has an offer, and it is low. You know they are going to be disappointed. First, you must know the facts regarding the buyer before you present the offer. You should call the agent and find out the story of the buyer. Why? Because you need to make them people to your seller. You should then let the agent know the offer is low and you will urge your client to counter. You have now set the expectation to the buyer's agent to expect a counter so they can prepare their buyer. If the buyer is asking for closing costs, you should also ask the question of what is more important to their buyer, the price or closing costs. This is important information for you to have when presenting.

Once you have gathered all the information and set the stage with the buyer's agent, you then can present it to the seller.

> *Sam, I received an offer on your property and I want to go over a few things with you. Now, I believe the offer is low, but I have already had a conversation with the buyer's agent and let them know there will more than likely be a counteroffer. Their offer is $_____ and they would like to close in 30 days with a ten-day inspection period. I found out that the buyers are moving here from California because their home burned down in the last round of fires. They are currently staying with family and literally have the clothes on their back. They love your home and feel it would be a comfortable place to rebuild their lives. Being from California, their agent said they put in their offer expecting us to counter because that is how things are done there. I would be happy to share my thoughts on a number for you to counter with or you can tell me yours. Which would you like? My thought is this; based on the property only being on the market a week, I feel you can lower your price by $5,000 and accept the rest of their terms. They*

*may negotiate one more time and I feel we still have a little room for them to do that. I wouldn't recommend accepting more than $10,000 off the price by the end of the negotiation. What are your thoughts?*

*There are a couple more things we need to factor in. They have ten days to conduct the inspection on the property. There are always things that come up on the inspection no matter how well you have maintained the home. When we receive their request of items to be repaired, I first send the request to one of our recommended contractors to give us a quote on all requests. Then I present it to you with how much things will cost. At that point, you and I will discuss what you are okay with fixing and what you don't want to fix. I don't want you to worry about this part of the process, but I do want you to know what to expect. Because we are in the inspection period for ten days, I would like to still have your open houses and allow backup offers. Are you okay with that? Do you have any questions about what to expect? Are you in agreement for the counter price and all other terms? I will write the counter and send it right over to you for your signature.*

In this scenario, we have prepared the agent for a counter, prepared our client for the possibility of further negotiation, set the expectation of the inspection period, and received confirmation to continue marketing the property for another ten days. Have we left anything open to catch our client off guard?

Absolutely not! Not only that, our client more than likely feels compassion for the buyer based on their story and will naturally feel good about selling the property that has been their home to a buyer that will love and care for their home as much as the seller did.

The art of negotiation is not about winning. It is about finding a common ground where both parties have had to give a little in order to gain the desired outcome. There have been times where I have had to explain this process to my opponent in order to gain an understanding of compromise. By setting expectations up front, you alleviate the possibility of surprise, therefore paving the way for a successful compromise. Your clients will feel comforted and understood as you prepare them for what is to come. Rarely will you have an obstacle that cannot be overcome when you understand your opponent, set expectations with both sides, and confirm the information agreed upon. After using the steps in common practice, you will see a pattern of using these steps in everyday life. The art of negotiation is all around us and with practice, you will become a master.

# 10

# Overcoming Objections and Closing Sequences

In Sales, one must master the art of overcoming objections and closing sequences. Every sales career requires the techniques you will learn in this chapter for optimum success. There are what I call "obvious" closes, and there are what I prefer to call "psychological" closes. Anybody can learn obvious closes; however only true masters of their craft utilize psychological closes. In this chapter, you will learn several techniques and the psychology behind why we use them.

## Conscious Vs. Unconscious Successful

The goal is to bring you to a "conscious" successful in sales so that you can repeat your success over and over again. An "unconscious" successful is a person that has success but doesn't know why. Sales is filled with peaks and valleys for several reasons. Valleys are when you plateau in your number of closings, lead generation, or a combination of both. A conscious successful can determine why they are successful but can also determine if they have gotten off track with their techniques and can fix their process easily in order to pull themselves out of their valley. Unconscious successfuls will make excuses for their valleys. They will not review their techniques and adjust back to what was making them successful. It is not uncommon for salespeople in general to become complacent and lazy with their techniques and steps to the sale. The conscious successful will keep themselves in check and revert back to what was making them successful.

Not everybody is cut out for a sales career. Some need the safety and security of knowing what they will make each month. People who thrive in their sales career are those that realize their income is dictated by their knowledge and dedication to their career and clients. The conscious successful chooses to master their craft by studying and staying on track with their closing sequences. Only you can choose which one you will be; the unconscious successful who bobs up and down in the water, struggling for air, or the conscious successful who always has a life raft to hold on to.

## Overcoming Objections

Objections are the reasons people come up with to avoid making a buying decision. There are "surface" objections, which are the easy, free flowing ones to uncover. An example of a surface objection is: "I still have to do more research before I buy anything." Typically, surface objections are predetermined and sometimes scripted by the client. We call them surface objections because they are simply that! They are simple objections to keep you from finding out what their real feelings and reasons are.

The second type of objections are "rooted" objections. They are the true objections that are attached to your client's real fears. Rooted objections are the objections you need to uncover. They are the ones you need to be able to overcome. If you are unable to uncover rooted objections, you are pretty much dead in the water.

The goal in overcoming objections is to "funnel" your client down to a buying decision. When you first meet them, there may be twenty surface objections. The goal is to get them to the one rooted objection so that you can ease their mind and fix the problem. You must find the "problem" that you need to fix, or you have no direction to go with your client. Fixing their problem, or easing their fears, is what builds your value to them. As each surface objection is brought up by your client, you tackle it, confirm it is no longer an issue, and move on to the next one. This phenomenon will take place throughout steps one through seven in your sales process. From the point of meeting your potential client through information confirmation in step seven, you were naturally overcoming objections in order to gain commitment for continued contact. Below are techniques and sequences that will help you get there.

## The Takeaway

I am asked all the time what a "takeaway" is. Before you understand what a takeaway is, you must first understand the psychology behind it. The takeaway works well with "Drivers" and "Analyticals!" The reason is because these personality types need to feel in control of their outcome and decisions.

Psychologically, the takeaway allows buyers to feel in control even though you are directing their decisions with your words. People always want what they can't have, especially a Driver! If you are having challenges keeping an "Expressive" in the picture, a takeaway will help as well.

The key to a takeaway is taking something off the table but then giving it back. Years ago, in timeshare sales, my job was to get my customers to the point of opening their mind. In our script, we specifically said, "my only request is that you keep an open mind and have some fun with me." If my customers were unwilling to act on my request, I used a form of takeaway that worked every time. I would take my presentation book off the table and sit it on the chair next to me. The customers always looked at me shocked and would ask what I was doing. My response was always the same, "I may be wrong, and you will have to tell me if I am, but it seems you don't want to hear about our program. We have 90 minutes to spend together so I am happy to speak about whatever you would like for our 90 minutes. Again, I may be wrong, you will have to let me know if you would like to learn more about our program." The customers would always look at me straight in the eyes and ask me to explain our program to them.

This is a very blatant, direct take away example. Let's break this down so you can understand what just happened. By me taking the presentation book off of the table, I took the option of learning more away. I followed it up with stating what I was taking away but then gave it back in the way I wanted them to answer by letting me know, they did, in fact want to learn more. I basically made them sell me on the idea of presenting to them.

Let's put this to practical use as it pertains to real estate. You have a potential client walk into your open house. You move through the first seven steps and offer to set up a property search. All of a sudden, you find out their objection is they will not be ready to purchase for another year, or maybe at least several months. They do not want to give you their information because they are not ready yet. Most real estate agents would give up at this point and let the potential client leave, but not the real estate agent who has mastered their craft of overcoming objections! The conscious successful real estate agent would use a takeaway! "Hmm, I have an idea. Now, this may work for you and it may not, you will have to let me know. It sounds like you are trying to get familiar with the market. I have met a lot of people in your shoes. What I did for them was set them up on a search they received once a week, just for them to keep getting educated on the market. Once they were ready to look more seriously, we increased their searches, but not until then. So, again, I don't know if this interests you, but I am willing to set up a search for you if you would like?" Are you able to see where I took it away and then gave it back?

Just recently I had to use this technique on a seller that was being unreasonable with their listing. The clients were being rude to my team members. I sent them an email that might shock many of you:

"Dear *John and Sue*,

It has come to my attention that you seem unhappy with my team's process for open houses. It is perfectly understandable as we are not like traditional realtors that you are used to. It crossed my mind that we may not be the right team to sell your home. Having sold 97 properties in your area this year alone, I believe we have proven our system works; however, I also understand we are not for everybody. Please let me know if I am wrong and you would like to move forward with us.

Sincerely,

Tina Valiant"

Most realtors would be too afraid to send an email such as this, but guess what? The client emailed me back and wanted to continue their listing with us. Please note that I also set the stage that we are in control and the expert in our business. We know what we are doing and treating my team badly will not be acceptable! This is a great technique for training clients on how you require to be treated.

Another example of a takeaway is for the client you are sending searches to and they are not responding, but you can see they are opening them. This takeaway works very well in text:

"Hello Sue. I have set up your searches just as we agreed to and I have been sending you handpicked searches as well. I have sent you emails and texts with no reply back, which leads me to believe you are not as ready to find a home as you originally lead me to believe. I may be wrong and if so, you will have to let me know you would like to continue. Unless I hear from you, I will stop sending searches until you are ready."

The agents on my team utilize this takeaway all the time and 80% of the time they receive a response back from their client apologizing for their lack of response and that they are ready to begin looking at properties. The 20% that do not respond, we follow through with discontinuing their searches because they have clearly decided to go a different direction. Takeaways are fantastic for weeding out the time wasters!

## Feel, Felt, Found

Why do we use a technique like "Feel, Felt, Found?" Because we are overcoming an objection by empathizing with one's feelings, explaining that others have felt the same way, and giving them facts through other's experiences. Feel, Felt, Found is a technique that has been used for years upon years. The technique has been around for so long that I cannot track down who first came up with it. I am going to give you some examples of how this technique works so that you can utilize it effectively to assist in overcoming your client's objections. Below is an example of the technique:

"Mr. Smith, I completely understand how you feel about not wanting to bother anybody with showing you properties while you are conducting your research. I have had other clients who have felt the same way as you.

What they found was by allowing me to assist them with at least their property searches, I was able to save them more time with their research by providing them with information that was exactly what they were looking for. Do you believe this would help you as well?"

**Feel -** You can see in the example given that the potential client's feelings are acknowledged. By acknowledging their feelings or thoughts, you are showing them that you are listening.

**Felt -** The "felt" portion exists to show the potential client they are not different than others. This portion of the technique gives the potential client peace of mind and demonstrates that they are not alone.

**Found –** The "found" portion of the conversation exists to give the potential client facts but not as YOU are telling them from your perspective. It is you sharing what OTHERS have found that are just like them.

The example below is an email that was sent by one of my agents on the team recently to a potential client. I helped my agent construct this email to battle the economy objection:

"Jane,

I completely understand your concern with buying a property now with looming talks of the economy falling in the next couple of years. I have had many other clients share in your concern and we have conducted research together in order to feel more confident with their buying decision. I am not an expert, but this is what the experts are saying here and what my clients have brought to my attention: Maricopa county has 263 people moving to the county per day. We have more accredited colleges being built than anywhere else in the country. Maricopa County has more technology jobs being created than anywhere else in the country. Arizona has more sports teams and events coming into our area on a consistent basis than other parts of the country. Our unemployment rate is at an all-time low and companies are having a hard time finding valued employees to fill open positions with their companies. Because of all of these facts, experts are saying that a dip in the economy is less likely to impact Arizona's economy compared to other parts of the country. Based on all of this information, as well as prices continuing to rise while inventory continues to fall, my past clients have found this to be a sound investment for their future. This may speak to you, it may not, you will have to let me know if the facts regarding the Arizona economy help ease your mind."

Always remember to follow up your "Feel, Felt, Found with a call to action or a closing question. This technique can be partnered with other techniques such as the "Take Away", "Third Party Stories", and "Closing Sequences." Once you master the technique, you will begin playing with the words depending on who is in front of you and what Personality Profiling type they are. You will also begin realizing how many times others use this technique on you to persuade you into making decisions.

## Third Party Stories

Third party stories are utilized to help ease your client's mind. Salespeople make the mistake of giving their own opinion and many times it backfires. With third party stories, it is other people's experiences that you are sharing. You must use third party stories that relate to your clients and what they are going through. Recently, I was showing a popular floor plan to a client that did not like the galley kitchen in the back of the house. I utilized feel, felt, found with a third-party story to help the client see another perspective:

> "Dan and Jill, I completely understand how you feel, many of my clients have felt the same way, and this is what several have found and expressed to me. Because this is the only split floor plan, three-bedroom model, they agreed to give the galley kitchen a try. My client Sally, who was just like you, called me the other day and was expressing how she misjudged having the galley kitchen in the back. She said she loves that guests cannot see her dirty dishes when they enter the home and then never need to go into the kitchen unless she invites them. She had considered opening the kitchen up but now can't imagine not having the kitchen set up the way it is because of the spacious counter tops and ease of entertaining. Based on her experience, it has really changed my mind about this kitchen. I don't know about you, but her experience has been wonderful, and

she absolutely loves the split floor plan. What are your thoughts?"

My clients, Dan and Jill, took Sally's experience into consideration and decided she had some valid points. They moved forward with purchasing the home and later reported exactly the same experience that I had shared with them.

By using third party stories, you are not coming off as trying to sell anybody anything. You are simply sharing other's experiences to give them different perspectives. If you simply shared your thoughts, your clients may feel as though you are just trying to sell them. Nobody likes to be sold something they are not sure of. They will however, identify with others that are like them. If you personally have an experience that you need to share, put it into a third-party story as somebody else's experience. You do not need to give names and falsify the story. You simply alleviate that the person in the third-party story is you.

## Closing Sequences

Utilizing takeaways, feel, felt, found, and third-party stories to funnel your client down will help you uncover and overcome rooted objections. Once funneled down, you must use closing sequences to bring the client to a final yes decision. Closing sequences utilize a combination of overcoming objections techniques, tie downs, and hard closing questions. As you become a master of all these techniques, hard closes become less and less needed. It is not uncommon for my clients to ask me what the next step is in order to move forward rather than me asking them.

### The Tie Down

When using tie downs, what you are essentially doing is getting a mild confirmation to move forward, or as we call them, a "temperature check." Tie downs are simple confirming questions such as "what are your thoughts" or "do you agree with me?" When we deliver the story of the home at an open house, we use a tie down question to proceed. After you have finished step one, the meet and greet, you move on to explaining you are going to give the story of the home and set them free. At the end, you should be asking permission: "I am going to give you the story of the home and then set you free, is that okay?" The "is that okay" is your tie down. You are already training them to agree with you psychologically by getting their agreement for you to move forward. Every step of the sales process is not complete until a tie down is used to gain confirmation to move forward. If you do not gain confirmation to move forward, you have a lot more work to do and should not move forward until you have the agreement to do so.

Tie downs are a non-invasive technique to gauge where your client is mentally. That is why we call them temperature checks. The goal is to unconsciously train your client to communicate and oftentimes, objections will come out during your tie down questions. You want as many objections to come out as possible because you cannot overcome something you do not know is there! Tie downs are a necessary part of your steps in funneling your clients down. There is nothing worse than getting broadsided after spending hours with a client, only to realize you never uncovered their rooted objections! Tie downs will avoid time wasting and uncover the rooted objections you need to know in order to proceed and overcome them.

## The "Hard" Close

The word "hard" in this section is not equal to difficult. It means asking a closing question such as "is this the home for you?" Another example of a hard close is "would you like to make an offer today?" Hard closes are not temperature checks. They are used when you are looking for a final answer. An example of a hard close that I despise is "what can I do to earn your business today?" This is the perfect example of a beginner sales question that oozes desperation and "rookie" all over it! Please do not be this type of salesperson! Now that I have pointed this specific question out, you will hear salespeople ask this question on a regular basis.

With hard closes, the key is knowing the timing and that you have earned the right to ask them. We call this being decently bold, which means earning the right to ask tough questions without fear of offending another. Hard closes should only be asked when you have built commonality, gained trust, and overcome objections. Let's say that a potential client walks into your open house. You move through setting them free and when they return you ask "so what do you think? Are you ready to make an offer?" I don't know about you, but I would be completely turned off by this! Now, let's say you have gone through steps one through seven. You have built commonality. The potential client is freely opening up to you. You have heard from them that they love this home, and it is everything they were hoping for. You have officially earned the right to ask, "well, it appears from what you are telling me, this is the home for you? I hope I am not being too bold by asking this, but would you like to maybe make an offer on this home?" Do you see the difference? One is hard, cold and pushy. The other is confirming and sensitive yet decently bold.

## Overcoming Objections and Closing Sequences in Action

I have added several scenarios below as examples for all of the techniques shared in this chapter. My best advice is to record yourself saying them and practice out loud how you sound. The last thing anybody wants is a salesperson who is scripted. You have to learn to make these sample scripts your own! You need to pay specific attention to what technique is being utilized in each scenario so that they become second nature to you. Most of this will feel very uncomfortable at first, which goes in line with a line I am well known for; "I will first make you uncomfortable before I make you successful." As you practice and the sequences and techniques become second nature to you, the sequences will flow out of you as if they have always been there. Always remember, clients cannot tell you yes if you do not first ask them the hard questions. You are not an advisor or tour guide. You are a closer! As a bonus, I have added my listing closing techniques as well for you.

## Open House Close:

After your steps of the Story of the Home and Setting Them Free with the Survey, once they come back to the table to give you the survey and clipboard, follow this sequence:

*So, what did you think about the home?* (Let them talk and do not interrupt!)

*What are you looking for?* (Write down everything they say)

*Do you have anybody helping you with your search?*

*What is your timeframe?*

*We can go look at properties today after my open house or tomorrow at _______ time.* ***Which one works better for you?*** (closing questions)

Make sure you allow them to speak as you ask them questions. Do not interrupt them and do not stop the conversation yourself! Leave your limiting beliefs at the door and allow them to open up to you.

## Open House Objections:

### I have an agent.

*That's wonderful! I am glad you found somebody you like and trust. Keep my information and if, for any reason, it does not work out for you, please call me.*

**I am just looking.**

*I completely understand. Is moving to this area something you are considering down the road? We have a lot of people checking things out for a potential move later. (pause) I have an idea, it may work for you and it may not. You will have to let me know, but one of the things I have done for other people in the area that want to get more educated on the market had me set a once a week search for them, again for educational purposes to help them make a decision down the road. I am not sure if you would be interested, but I am happy to set the same kind of search up for you? Education is a big part of figuring out if and when you want to move.* ***Would you like me to set that up for you?*** (This is a hard close with a takeaway. Shut up and listen to them)

**I'm a neighbor and wanted to stop in and check things out.**

*You know, it is funny, I have a lot of neighbors in today! One of your neighbors was in earlier today and was telling me that she likes to come into open houses to look at the different floor plans and possibly remodeling ideas. She explained to me that she isn't fond of her floor plan. How do you feel about yours?* (Third party story to draw out information and plant the seed of doubt about their own floor plan)

**Buyer's Appointments:**

Show different homes and let them give you feedback on each one. Take mental notes on everything they say and confirm their thoughts and feelings. If you are in a home they seem to love, it is time to close them:

*Wow, this home does have (confirm what they said as they were walking through), it also has (explain some of the other things that were on the list they originally told you). What do you think? Do we need to look at more or is this the one? (Hard close)*

If their response is: "No, we want to look at more."

*Alright, I have (state how many you have to look at today) to see today. If we don't find "the one" we can go out again tomorrow, but we may need to change some of the things on your "wants" list. Inventory is limited, as I explained before, this one has been on the market (number of days on market). We can always come back and take a second look at this one after viewing the other properties. Is that fair?* (This is a tie down question)

If their response is: "Yep, this is it!"

*Great! I am so glad we found the right home for you! Let's discuss the offer you would like me to put together for you. The home has been on the market (number of days on market). The price point is good. I am going to have to call the agent to see if they have received other offers currently. It is very common to be in a multiple offer situation in today's market. My suggestion, however, I will write it how you want me to, is to give them a strong offer. What number are you thinking?* (Hard close)

**Listing Closes:**

After the tour of the property, there is a sequence of closing and gaining commitments.

*Thank you for showing me your home and having me over today. Let me show you what my comps say and then we will go over my thoughts on what your home is worth. Is that fair?* (This is a tie down statement)

Before proceeding to the numbers, ask them their plans for when this house sells.

*Before we dive into the numbers, I must first ask you a question to make sure we are on the same page. When this house sells, what is your plan? I always like to make sure I understand your plan so that I can better assist you.*

Present the numbers based on the comps, tell them your thoughts on what you are coming in at for list price.

*(Their Name), one of the biggest things I look at in pricing your house is the amount and types of upgrades you do or do not have. Based on viewing your home you have (list upgrades or lack of upgrades). Would you*

*agree with me on everything I just stated? Because of these factors, I feel your home is worth $___________. This number is based on what has sold in your area in the past six months that is comparable to your property. What are your thoughts/feelings based on what I have explained?* (You must have complete confidence when presenting the numbers. If you are not confident, they will feel your uneasiness and follow suit.)

**If they agree with your price opinion:**

*I'm glad we are on the same page!* (Move to the next closing questions)

**If they do not agree:**

*Ok, I hear what you are saying, what were you hoping for?* (shut up and listen)

*Why were you hoping for that number?* (shut up and listen)

Run the numbers based on square footage and determine if we can come close to what they were hoping for.

*Based on square footage, because that is how appraisers look at properties in this area, price per square foot depending on upgrades, I feel we cannot go higher than $_________. The reason is because my job is not only to get you the most money for your property, but also in most cases, unless it is a cash offer, I also have to make sure I can get the property to appraise. You would be* *pretty upset if I sold your property and we couldn't get it to appraise for the offer amount, wouldn't you agree? (Tie down) I say we start at $___________, test the market and see what kind of response we get. If we are not getting showing requests, then we will know we are priced too high and need to adjust in a couple of weeks. Are you okay with my suggested strategy?* (Tie down)

**Showing the numbers broken down:**

*Let me show you a couple of different scenarios of offers so you can see what you will net, because at the end of the day, that is what matters most. Would you agree?* (Tie down)

Write down an offer amount of what you are listing for. Subtract 6% realtor commissions from the gross proceeds and show the total underneath. Then subtract 1% for estimated closing costs. *Do you have a loan on the property? If so, how much do you owe?* If they have a loan, subtract the estimated payoff amount from the total. Circle the bottom number and write NET next to it. Do the same math with an offer for $10,000 less than the listed price amount. Once you have completed both scenarios, turn the paper around and explain both to them. Examples are below:

| | |
|---|---|
| Listing price | $199,900 |
| Gross offer amount | $195,000 |
| Realtor commissions 6% | -$11,700 |
| | $183,300 |
| Estimated closing costs 1% | $1,950 |
| | $181,350 |
| Loan amount | $0 |
| NET | $181,350 |

| | |
|---|---|
| Gross offer amount | $185,000 |
| Realtor commissions 6% | -$11,100 |
| | $173,900 |
| Estimated closing costs 1% | -$1,850 |
| | $172,050 |
| Loan amount | $0 |
| NET | $172,050 |

*I want you to have a good idea of range when we receive offers.* Point to higher offer amount and go down the list explaining each item. When you get to commissions state it this way. *This is all realtor commissions, meaning if another agent outside of our team sells your home, they will receive 3% and we will receive 3%. The next item is the estimated closing costs, which could be a little higher or a little lower depend-*

*ing on prorations. So, after all expenses are paid out, this is what you will put in your pocket. How do you feel/think about that number?* (Tie down. Get confirmation or you cannot proceed!!!!!)

**Hard Close**

> *When would you like for me to get the property on the market?* (Please note I said property and not home as to disassociate from the property)

**They are ready now or next week**

Get confirmation by repeating back to them what they said to you. *Ok, right away, let's get everything scheduled.* Move to next step

**They are not ready, and you need to uncover the rooted objection:**

> *I understand you are not ready quite yet, which tells me you are having some hesitations on selling your property and when. May I ask what your concerns are? This helps me to help you better.* (Shut up and listen and let them puke all over you! Do not start talking until they are done.) After they have finished sharing their concerns, handle each objection one by one confirming their thoughts and feelings and presenting solutions. Remember, a problem is not a problem if there is a solution! After you overcome each objection one by one, you can ask them; *So, we have covered all of your concerns (list each concern again with the solution), are*

*you more comfortable now to move forward and set a date for listing the property?* (Hard close. Remember in this moment you have nothing to lose and everything to gain. If you walk out that door without a firm commitment, you will more than likely lose the listing to the next person that walks in the door. Are you willing to lose it because of fear of hearing no?) *Wonderful, I have a listing contract here that is blank that I can fill out.*

## Schedule Neighbors Only Party

*I need to schedule your neighbors only party and photos. We typically do them on Thursday from 3-5 and we flyer around the neighborhood with invites for the neighbors to preview the home prior to the property officially being on the market. We do this for two reasons, first the neighbors will come anyway so we would rather get them all out of the way at the same time so that we can focus on real buyers over the weekend. The second reason to conduct neighbors only parties is because the neighbors know people that want to buy in their neighborhood. They will bring potential buyers back to us. Does Thursday from 3-5 work for you. We prefer for you not to be here.* (Hard close. Get confirmation on dates and times that work. We do neighbors only parties typically on Thursdays 3-5)

## Schedule Photos, sign and lock box

*I would like to take photos right away so that we are ready to get on the market.* ***Which morning works best for you or is afternoon better?***

## Schedule Open Houses

*What is your availability for open houses? Our open houses are 10-2 and I can do them Thursdays through Sundays. The most important days are weekends. Can we start this weekend to hit the ground running on your first weekend on the market? Who knows, we may get multiple offers. If we do, then I will let all of the buyer's agents know that we are not answering offers until Monday at 5:00 p.m. I will then present them all to you at once, so we can pick the best offer. Does that sound like a good plan to you?* (Tie down. Get confirmation on open houses that minute and set the expectation)

As you are leaving, make sure you confirm all commitment times. Do not leave any stone unturned with firm commitment on every item! Let your clients know you will be emailing them a copy of their executed listing agreement for their records.

There are a multitude of ways to uncover and handle objections, as well as creating different closing sequences that fit your market and personality. This chapter has been education to open your mind to the psychology behind why we say the things we do, funneling a client down to a yes, and sifting out timewasters. Once the above techniques are mastered, you will be ready to begin creating your own closing sequences. A true master never stops improving their craft! At the end of each day, you should recap the different scenarios you came across and how the techniques you used worked for you. If your technique was very effective, you should write it down to remind yourself in the future.

Being a conscious successful means being able to retrace your steps and fix your techniques in the midst of a valley. Even the most experienced salespeople can become lazy and complacent with their techniques and steps in their sales process. If you find yourself in a valley where day after day you are not closing the same amount of clients or gaining commitment as you once did, it is time to go back to what made you successful before. Your overcoming objections and closing sequences techniques will change over time, however there is no denying the basics and foundation of what always works. With the knowledge you have gained in this chapter, you will always have a base to go back to when needed.

# 11

# Keeping Your Clients for Life

After the close of a property, agents tend to forget about their clients and move on to the next prospects. I did not want to believe this to be true until I began asking our listing appointments who sold them their homes originally. Our potential client's answers were astounding! Most people I asked couldn't remember their agent's name. If the potential clients did remember their previous agent's name, the potential clients would tell me they never heard from their agent again after the closing of their property. They didn't have the agent's contact information or know whether the agent was still in the business!

I have given what I call "epic failure" on the part of the agents a lot of thought. We work so hard to procure clients and close transactions, why would we not continue to foster those relationships? It doesn't take a lot of effort to pick up the phone and check in our past clients. I tried to think of fears that might be behind the negligence of following up on and staying in contact. The reality is, there isn't a fear large enough to prevent an agent from staying in contact with past clients! The only thing I could come up with was laziness.

There should be regular follow up with your past clients for several reasons. Eventually, they are going to sell their property. Another reason is they have friends and family buying and selling property. If you stay in contact, you will stay at the forefront of their mind. When anybody asks them who they recommend in Real Estate, you will automatically come to mind.

Our clients, biggest fear is that real estate agents do not care about them. All the agent wants is the commission. When we close on their transaction and never check in on them, we are proving their fear to be true. We are saying subconsciously "thank you for the commission and good luck to you!" The agents who have long-term success are those that build a referral-based business because of their continued relationship with their past clients.

One of the questions I am asked regularly by newer agents and sometimes experienced agents I how to follow up appropriately. I teach my agents on my team to pick up the phone regularly starting with a week after the closing. The conversation should be free flowing backed by excitement.

*"Hello Sue. I just wanted to take a moment to check in on you and make sure you moved in okay. How is everything going with your new home?"*

Your clients will be delighted to hear from you and feel you care about them. You should remind them in your first follow up call and every call after, that if they ever need anything done to the home, you have several professionals you can recommend to them. It is not uncommon for our clients to reach out to us months to years later asking if we know of a plumber, roofer, or another type of vendor that we could recommend to them. This fact alone is why our professional referral partner list is so important. You want to set yourself apart as a one stop phone call for anything your past clients might need. Being the connected professional they can count on will keep them calling for years to come.

After your first week follow up, you should be contacting them every three months to check in on them as people. Your calls do not need to be real estate related.

*"Hello Sue, the holidays are coming up and you crossed my mind. Any big plans for the holidays this year?"* You can see that I'm not asking them about the house at all. I am checking in with them as people and taking an interest in their life. People want to know that you care about them. They need to feel that you are genuine. If there is an important date coming up like an anniversary or birthday, send them a handwritten card. Greeting cards have become a lost art.

Have you received a greeting card from a professional that seems sweet but at the bottom it states, "Thank you for your referrals" and has a business card inside? Does this cheapen the experience because their clear purpose is asking for more business? Don't be that person! There is no need to tell them you want referrals or send them a business card if you are always in the forefront of their mind. You will gain more referrals from them if you show them you care about them. Your past clients will never think of using somebody else or recommending somebody that isn't you as long as you are genuine and keep an interest in them.

As we learned in Chapter 4, "Building a Relationship Based Business" referrals are gold. Your closing ratios are much higher in regard to referrals. Doesn't it make sense to put the time in to fostering your past client relationships just as much as the time you are spending on finding new clients? Referrals close at a 90% ratio whereas new potential clients can be as low as 10%. It takes much less time overall to foster your referral network! As long as you follow up with a phone call every quarter, send handwritten greeting cards for holidays and special occasions, and stay in the forefront of their mind, your business will explode with referrals!

You should have a customer relations management system, also known as a CRM. Your past clients should be on a monthly drip campaign giving them an update on their neighborhood sales and the value of their home. Having your clients on a drip campaign does not replace your responsibility to call them and send cards. The drip campaign is not the personal touch your past clients are seeking. Relying on your drip campaign will not set you apart from anybody else. Your goal is to be different and for your past clients to see you as such.

Over time, your efforts will be rewarded with your phone ringing. Your follow up with your past clients will become more fruitful than any other activities you can spend your time on. Do not be like thousands of lazy agents out there who close and forget. Be the star agent who eventually only works with referrals because you kept in contact with your past clients and treated them like people, not just a dollar sign.

# 12

## YOU ARE READY TO SOAR

There is a great book called "The Traveler's Gift" by Andy Andrews that I recommend everybody read. The book has Seven Decisions to live by. In Decision 2: The Guided Decision; I will seek wisdom, Andrews gives a great analogy of surrounding yourself with people that are going places:

*"I will seek wisdom. I will choose my friends with care. I am who my friends are. I speak their language, and I wear their clothes. I share their opinions and their habits. From this moment forward, I will choose to associate with people whose lives and lifestyles I admire. If I associate with chickens, I will learn to scratch at the ground and squabble over crumbs. If I associate with eagles, I will learn to soar to great heights. I am an eagle. It is my destiny to fly."*

The biggest failure of the real estate industry is the lack of actual sales training designed for real estate agents. Most get into the real estate business believing they will make their own schedules and all of their friends and family will buy from them. Nobody decides on a real estate career believing it is a sales position that is going to take a lot of work!

To sum up what you have learned in this book; You are in sales! You now have the foundation and tools to set yourself apart in this industry. Mastering your craft of real estate sales will take time, patience, and a lot of continued practice. Choosing to read this book is your first step in soaring with the eagles!

The 16 steps to the sales process is your roadmap for success. Everything else in this book is the meat between the bones. The meat is what helps you succeed at your goals personally and professionally. The psychology behind the sale is a huge part of the meat and is what keeps your clients coming back for more!

You have learned how to properly set expectations throughout the transaction, how to break down barriers, and show your clients you are different from other agents out there. Most importantly, you have learned how to express to your clients that you are their friend and will protect them, sometimes from themselves.

I am receiving feedback from all over the country that my 16 steps work. The open house strategies, overcoming objections, and closing sequences work! You have been armed with the knowledge and skills to be successful in real estate! Now, it is up to you to master the concepts you have learned and put them into action. You've got this! Go be an eagle so that you can show others how to soar as well!

# Author Bio

About Tina Valiant

Professionals in the Real Estate industry know award-winning real estate agent, author, speaker, and Real Estate Coach, Tina Valiant, as a dynamic sales star and master negotiator who builds award-winning teams and has saved hundreds of homeowners and investors from foreclosure. The Arizona based Real Estate agent didn't become the outspoken and inspiring coach that she's known as today, overnight.

From being voted least likely to succeed in timeshare sales, being told she would never succeed in residential real estate sales and having to overcome some of life's toughest medical circumstances, to transforming herself into the number one sales agent year after year, and leading one of Phoenix, Arizona's top real estate teams (which she built from the ground up), Tina Valiant is no stranger to overcoming life's obstacles and the power of personal transformation. Tina developed *Relationship Real Estate* originally for her team and because of their overwhelming success she decided to share her knowledge and training with other agents across the country.

She began the journey of finding her voice in 2001 as a shy housewife and stay-at-home-mom and has since transformed into an industry icon most known for her proven approach to coaching agents through their limiting beliefs, personal issues, and roadblocks that prevent sales teams from experiencing ultimate success. She currently resides in Arizona and has two adult daughters. Tina is also the author of *Finding Your Voice*, a personal development book. She speaks to audiences of all sizes and teaches two-day workshops all over the country.

Made in the USA
Columbia, SC
22 September 2024